To my mum Elena, babushka Lida, babushka Liana,
and our ancestors, for standing in the kitchen with me.

SOUR CHERRIES & SUN FLOWERS

RECIPES FROM EASTERN EUROPE AND BEYOND

Photography by Karen Fisher and Anastasia Zolotarev

Quadrille

Contents

Introduction

Growing up, I didn't think twice about the food of my family. It's not that I didn't enjoy it but I ate to feel full, and quickly too. I never took a moment to notice the smells, colours, textures, how it was made or the reasons why. I saw food preparation as a chore: setting the table, peeling potatoes, picking mushrooms, filling cabbage leaves, folding dumplings... the list goes on.

It was years before I understood how special the food of my heritage is. Now I actively embrace opportunities to cook borsch, to set up the table with two days' worth of preparation, to cook with my mum and babushka, to feed others, to eat together or go foraging. Making meals is a precious part of daily life; it reveals who we are, because of how we live, or how our families once lived. Writing this book has caused me to reflect on the moments that occur when preparing food, together or alone, quickly or slowly, in winter or summer. It has provided a space to gather places, people, their stories and food. My family recipes represent decades of cooking and eating, connecting past and present, and continuing – or evolving – traditions.

Sour Cherries and Sunflowers is a celebration of the joy in all of this. Whenever I eat a sour cherry, if I close my eyes, I'm back at my late babushka Lida's *dacha* (summerhouse), where sour cherry trees flourish in the backyards of her old village in Baranavichy, western Belarus. This is where I was born. Equally, when I see, smell or taste sunflower oil, I am instantly transported to Ukraine – my dad's home – where we lived for five years with my Ukrainian grandparents before we emigrated to Australia. At the time, these ingredients were not available in Australia, so whenever I returned to Eastern Europe I would search for them. In summer, buckets of sour cherries are sold by locals on the roadside and bottles of golden, unrefined sunflower oil are often for sale outside someone's house; I'd ask to stop the car whenever I spotted any. Happily, I can now source both in Sydney, my new home; perhaps there's not the exact taste or feeling, but it's close enough.

It's a strange feeling to be at home in one place, with the home your family once knew so distant, physically and spiritually. At times I find myself wondering: What is happening on that street where I spent my first years? How is that neighbour who invited us in for coffee? And at babushka Liana's dacha that she and my grandfather built while I sat watching: What plants grow there now and is anyone caring for them?

We left Kharkiv, Ukraine, in 1994. Finding myself in Brisbane as a 6-year-old, my goal was to become 'Australian' as fast as possible. After a year, I had nearly caught up on the language and the clothes, but my school lunchbox was different and it gave away that I was from a far-off place few people had heard of, other than 'some country in the Soviet Union.' Mum, unaware of my goal of integration, used to make me gourmet sandwiches, say chicken pâté with cucumber, or a garlicky beetroot dip. I would scoff my lunch as quickly as possible; some days I didn't eat it at all, which I still feel guilty about. But understandably, no one can teach you how to shift between cultures. Now I want to celebrate the dishes Mum used to make, including her pâté, with which my 'hate–love' relationship has become one of complete love and appreciation.

Despite the strain of having to leave our place of birth, home and family, my book is not about the sadness of separation, or relinquishing an old life in search of a different one. When my parents and I came to Australia, it was an adventure – compared to what they experienced in the Soviet Union, particularly in the years leading up to their move – with a new level of freedom. It gave me cultural traditions in the ever-evolving city that is Sydney, where I found many friends who likewise came from other places. I had family in two continents and that made me feel both distant and connected at the same time.

My hope is that this book will inspire you to cook my family recipes and celebrate the food and flavours of Ukraine, Belarus and beyond. Food is grounding, it connects us to our culture and past through tradition, it moves with people, crosses borders, and is ever evolving. It provides a sense of home – take this as your invitation to mine.

A bit of context

I have always felt food is connected to surroundings, moments and often memory, which is the basis on which I have organized these recipes into chapters. When I had finished writing, I realized that many of the recipes and stories show a beautiful and romantic side to my heritage. Of course, some recipes that shaped my family's food were influenced by hardships from specific moments in history or the politics of the region at the time. That said, this book is not political, and the stories I share don't always reflect the full picture or history of a dish.

This book showcases the flavours of Eastern Europe – a region that's definition has changed over the years – through my personal lens. My family is of East Slavic origins. Growing up in a mixed Eastern European household in Kharviv, Ukraine, with a Ukranian dad and a Belarusian mum, we spoke Russian at home, as did many households during the time of the Soviet Union and after it's dissolution. So, you'll see this reflected in the following pages, as well as the influence of surrounding countries, such as Lithuania, Latvia, Poland, Romania and beyond. With the changing of borders and the movement of people, these unique cultures have each played a part in shaping the food of my family.

Throughout, I have attempted to incorporate some historical context by translating the recipe titles variously into Ukrainian, Belarusian or Russian, according to both the heritage of the dish and my personal experience of it. Many Eastern European countries have their own variations of a particular dish, so where possible, the language I have included reflects those origins.

I wish food was not political, but where my family are from, it was often used as a form of control. Access to food was so shaped by politics that there were times in my parents' and grandparents' lives that revolved around trying to source produce. Babushka Liana still remembers the hunger during certain periods of the Soviet Union. Ukraine was known for rich soils and producing diverse foods, and Belarus for natural resources in its forests and beyond. Yet the bulk of what was grown and harvested was taken away. A few decades ago family members queued for hours just to enter a store with barely anything to sell. Everyone had to be resourceful. People learnt how to cook with only a handful of ingredients, to waste nothing, and to grow, forage and preserve food. Importantly, they also celebrated it.

A whole book could be written on the political context of the recipes of this region and it's an incredibly complex history. This is my personal take on the food of my family. I hope that this serves as a starting point for your journey and gives some cultural background to the wonderful flavours of Eastern Europe.

How to cook from this book

There are two sayings that my family often use when it comes to cooking. When I was rediscovering these recipes, I asked, 'How much flour/sugar/ butter exactly?' Or 'For how long do I cook the cabbage/steam the wild blueberry dumplings?' I was met with a simple answer: '*na glazok*' – 'by the eye'. Then, when I'd finished cooking and testing the recipes, keen to ensure they'd work for anyone making them for the first time, I'd ask my family to try them. They would reply: 'Good but... *nada nabit' ruku*', which roughly translates as 'you need to warm up your hand', meaning to get the hang of cooking, shaping, rolling or feeling that only comes with practice. In other words, it's instinctive; it takes multiple goes before it's perfect. That's not my favourite word in cooking, though, because my idea of perfect is always different from someone else's. So I've written the recipes as if you were in the kitchen with me, my mum, my babushkas and others who have taught me so much about the food of my heritage. I give guidance and detail in the methods, but there are so many variables in cooking, it's for you to adjust as you feel, see and taste.

Introduction

An Eastern European Pantry

The foods, flavours and specialities of Eastern European cooking are so varied. I am sharing what is in my own pantry, directly inspired by my family's heritage. Many staple ingredients are easier and cheaper to make than buy, if you have the time, although for convenience most are found in Eastern European delis, and supermarkets stock certain items. I hope to surprise you with the accessibility of, or ease of, making these ingredients.

Vegetables

My family recipes are often influenced by seasonally grown vegetables. Here are some of them.

CABBAGE

Cabbages offer such versatility. Most shop-bought ones have the outer leaves removed, are cut in half and wrapped in plastic, resulting in less flavour and liquid with each passing day. Try asking for a whole cabbage, which will likely be kept in storage, until the shop-front produce has sold. A whole leafy cabbage has much more juice and flavour, and can make several meals. I use half for cabbage rolls and still have enough to sauté in butter with carrot and onion as a delicious side or filling. Use red or white cabbage for slaws and sauerkraut, and older cabbage to cook with.

POTATOES

When potatoes were first introduced to Eastern Europe, they grew well and provided a year-round food source, particularly in winter when other vegetables were scarce. In summer, new potatoes can be simply boiled and eaten topped with unrefined sunflower oil or butter and a sprinkle of salt – they also make a delicious salad. Older, larger potatoes are generally best for grating or roasting. I buy unwashed potatoes – they last longer and have more flavour. Store potatoes in a dark cupboard and avoid any that are green-tinged or soft.

An Eastern European Pantry

SALAD GREENS AND HERBS

Greens and herbs include lettuce, wild greens and spinach, spring onions, parsley, dill, tarragon and basil. To keep them fresh, wash greens well, then dry on paper towels. Store soft herbs in the refrigerator in jars half-filled with water, covered with a plastic bag – they last much longer. If they start to wilt, finely chop and freeze them to add to your cooking. Most herbs are easy to grow and can also be dried to add to ferments and pickles.

BEETROOTS AND RADISHES

Buy untrimmed whole beetroots and radishes. The leaves and stems are great additions to soups. Unpeeled beetroots are easy to cook in the oven, either directly on one of the shelves or in a tray of water. The skin contains flavour and colour so only peel if grating beetroots, say for sauerkraut (page 64), or to use raw in a slaw. They pair beautifully with apples and raw grated radishes or turnips. We often have fresh radishes as they are, topped with salt and golden unrefined sunflower oil. Store in the refrigerator.

MUSHROOMS

Most varieties are best simply sliced or chopped and added to your cooking or used for pickling. Certain types of wild mushrooms need soaking first (see page 75). For store-bought mushrooms like chestnut or button, brush off any soil or, if the skin doesn't look great, peel them and slice off the end of the stems. Fresh mushrooms can be dried at home and also freeze well (see pages 74–75). Porcini are available fresh, dried or frozen. If you can't find them locally, see the stockists on page 201.

CUCUMBERS

Cucumbers used to be much more bitter than they are now, one reason for fermenting and pickling with herbs and flavours – I found one family recipe for cucumbers dipped in honey! Fresh cucumbers, simply seasoned in salt and tossed with dill and oil, often feature on Eastern European tables. Firmer-skinned gherkins are best for pickling or fermenting.

TOMATOES

Try to source seasonal tomatoes in summer and early autumn. Small ones are great for pickles; larger, heirloom varieties for salads. Make a quick passata by grating ripe tomatoes, removing the skins and simmering in a saucepan until slightly reduced. Use this to add to preserves like the pickled cucumbers in tomato sauce (page 70) or to borsch (pages 125 and 127).

GARLIC AND ONION

Store whole garlic bulbs and onions in a dark cupboard. If you only use half an onion, put the other half in a jar in the refrigerator – it will last longer.

Fruits and berries

Stock your freezer with wild blueberries, blackcurrants, sour cherries and other berries and fruits to make quick jams and preserves (pages 60–89) or the drink known as Kompot (page 91). Dried ripe barberries (from speciality grocers and online) add a sweet tartness to dishes like Plov (page 140), and pitted prunes are ideal in slow-cooked stews or stuffed onions (page 100). We use sultanas too – try to find ones uncoated in oils.

Meats, broths and fats

Pork has always been the main meat used in Eastern European cooking; lamb and beef featured only occasionally, although this is changing. Likewise, chicken and duck were reserved for celebratory dishes but are now more common. Several recipes call for stock or broth, as Mum is always so passionate about making her own (see page 135).

PORK
Try to source full-fat pork mince or make your own, if you have a mincer, as my family often would. Mum recalls from her childhood that winter meant slaughtering the household pig, then preparing the different cuts: nothing was wasted. These days, in Eastern European markets, you'll find local specialties that make use of everything from nose to tail, including the blood. Often the meat is salted, dry-cured in spices and herbs, or smoked.

SALO (CURED PORK FAT)
Salo is salted fat, sometimes covered in herbs and spices. It's so easy to make (see page 82) and keep in the freezer, ready for use. It's often used for frying, be it pancakes or potatoes. For convenience, you can use Italian pancetta or lardo (sometimes) but salo is very different.

LAMB TALLOW/FAT
This is the traditional fat used to fry *plov* and *chebureky*. If you can find any, a little goes a long way. It's available from speciality butchers and online.

Fish

Salted herring is available from supermarkets, but the best is found in Eastern European delis; some even salt their own. A few recipes call for salmon; you can easily swap that for trout. I keep the skin on for flavour and natural fat while cooking. Salmon fish roe (red caviar) is often added to cold fish dishes and blini (Eastern European pancakes). Try a local fishmonger or the stockists on page 201.

An Eastern European Pantry

An Eastern European Pantry

An Eastern European Pantry

Dairy

Dairy is a staple, and many recipes use milk, yoghurt, smetana (soured cream), tvorog (a soft, dense cheese) and kefir to enrich doughs and dumplings, to add flavour, acidity or creaminess, or to soften the intensity and richness of soups.

BUTTER AND GHEE

We use butter for a lot of cooking. Mum often makes and uses ghee (a type of clarified butter) in her cooking, something cooks in Belarus do too. Use ghee to fry the *Chebureky* (Lamb Turnovers, page 105), *Pyrizhky* (Fried Hand Pies, page 114) and any of the stews.

KEFIR (FERMENTED MILK)

Kefir is drunk as is, used in cooking or stirred into soups. It's North Caucasian in origin, but widespread throughout Eastern Europe where, simply by leaving milk out overnight, it naturally ferments owing to the presence of wild yeasts and good bacteria in the air. Elsewhere it's made using kefir grains, which are readily available; I've included a recipe on page 148. Kefir is found in supermarkets and Eastern European delis.

SMETANA (SOURED CREAM)

Smetana in my family and in many Eastern European households is the equivalent of salt: it's used for EVERYTHING – and features in many of my recipes. There may be 20–30 varieties in stores across Eastern Europe, and local vendors sell their village-produced smetana, each slightly different in thickness and tang. Try to buy full-fat smetana.

TVOROG AND BRYNDZA

Tvorog (*syr* in Ukrainian, *tvaroh* in Belarusian) is best described as somewhere between curd cheese and cottage cheese. It's made by fermenting warm milk (usually cow's but I've seen buffalo's and sheep's milk versions) with special bacterial cultures found in yoghurt, and is quite different from quark, cottage cheese or other curd cheeses. Proper tvorog from Eastern European delis comes at a high price, so why not make your own (see recipe on page 81)? For convenience though, and when you need only a small amount, look to buy the drier style, which is more versatile and easy to cook with. If it's slightly wet, place in a muslin/cheesecloth-lined sieve and drain the whey into a bowl to use for things like *syrnyky* (page 30).

Bryndza is a tangy and salty sheep's milk cheese and it's basically like feta, which makes a good alternative. You can enjoy it as is, simply sliced and topped with raw honey, walnuts and fresh tarragon.

Oils, vinegars, condiments, preserves and ferments

These are key ingredients to cook with and to season dishes with sweet, salty, earthy, sour or acidic flavours.

SUNFLOWER OIL

Unrefined and refined sunflower oils are very different. Until recently it was hard to find golden unrefined sunflower oil outside Ukraine and Eastern Europe. Unrefined sunflower oil is a golden elixir, simply drizzled over boiled potatoes sprinkled with salt. The lighter, refined sunflower oil is more suitable for frying.

APPLE CIDER VINEGAR AND WHITE VINEGAR

Unfiltered or raw apple cider vinegar retains more flavour, is less processed and contains a live culture, or 'the mother'. It is less sweet too, I find, but preserves the beautiful apple flavour. We add it to so many dishes that call for vinegar. For a simple salad dressing, mix a splash of apple cider vinegar with some oil, a touch of honey and some salt – shake it well and pour over your salad. It's also used to make dough for savoury and sweet dishes.

White vinegar is used for pickling – use a regular-strength vinegar, around 3–4 per cent, for my pickling recipes. Anything stronger has a very intense flavour.

HONEY

Look for local raw honey if you can, one that is processed as naturally as possible. It will be rich in flavour and not overly sweet when used in cakes and dressings. Or source Ukrainian honey online: it's produced by bees that feed on wild flowers and sunflowers that lend a distinct flavour to the honey. Fresh, raw honey is golden, transparent and syrupy – this type is great to use in dressings – and, over time, its consistency changes to become set and firm.

SAUERKRAUT

Slightly aged sauerkraut is great for adding flavour to stews, soups and all manner of fillings. Fry it with fresh cabbage as a side dish. It's readily available, but check it's not sweetened and pasteurized – that's a very different product and I'd avoid it for cooking. Try to source one that is fermented, raw and salty, or make your own (see page 64).

An Eastern European Pantry

ADJIKA AND RED PEPPER PASTE

Adjika is made from red peppers fermented with herbs, garlic and salt. Dry adjika can also be found, but the recipes in this book use the paste form. My family use adjika a lot, so I've added a recipe for it (see page 78) to add to stews and soups for a boost of flavour and seasoning or to serve with meats. You can find more traditional versions of adjika online or in Eastern European or Georgian stores; I've provided a stockist for it too.

Red pepper paste, made from sun-dried red peppers, is used to add flavour in a similar way. We often use this instead of tomato paste.

Grains

Grains are central to Eastern European cooking because they grow so well in this part of the world. Rye and buckwheat flour feature prominently in my family recipes; some also use pearl barley or rice.

BUCKWHEAT

Look for toasted buckwheat, available in Eastern European delis or online. We never use raw dried buckwheat; it's a totally different product (I find it tasteless) and has to be soaked for 12 hours before cooking. Dry-toasted or roasted buckwheat has an almost nutty flavour – it's delicious freshly cooked then topped with butter and salt. We use it for stuffing meats, fillings, soups and as a base or side dish.

Seeds and nuts

Seeds and nuts are commonly used in Eastern European cooking to add to breads, cakes, and salads; we also make quick pestos out of some, such as the Walnut Pesto on page 42.

SUNFLOWER SEEDS

We used to grow sunflowers at my babushka Liana's dacha in Ukraine, where we'd dry the flowers then toast the seeds. Ukraine is one of the biggest producers of sunflowers, and the toasted seeds make the perfect snack! It's common in Eastern Europe to have salted toasted sunflower seeds with a cold beer.

WALNUTS

Walnuts are best bought in the shell as, once shelled, they can easily turn rancid and taste very bitter. Keep shelled walnuts, other nuts and seeds in the refrigerator in a tightly sealed jar.

Mornings

Mornings

Recipes to start the day

I love mornings, whatever the season. Opening the blinds to let the fresh air and light come through is a joy, whether waking up to the sounds of someone preparing breakfast or finding I'm the first one in the kitchen. Breakfast often involves butter, and the smell and sound of it sizzling on a cast-iron pan means we are cooking bread, eggs, mushrooms or pancakes of some sort. Buckwheat porridge, fried mushrooms or eggs are always my go-tos for a quick casual breakfast. The Ukrainian version of French toast, *hrinky*, is another family favourite that takes minutes to make.

On weekends or 'slow' mornings, I often cook something special like *oladya*, buckwheat yoghurt pancakes made with sliced apples and cinnamon, or *blinchiki* – Eastern European-style thin pancakes filled with tvorog and jam. Dairy products are very much central to this chapter, especially tvorog, which can be used to make *zapekanka* – semolina and cheese bake. See the recipe for making your own tvorog in the Preservation chapter, page 81.

Eastern European Pancakes

Blini

So often I have sat watching my mum make blini, asking her questions again and again, each time extracting more detail on her approach. Although it took her years to perfect her recipe, I think you can get these pretty close to hers, with *practice*. Use plain wheat or rye flour, spelt, buckwheat or a mix – even throw in some sourdough starter, whey or kefir that you might want to use up. Depending on the flour you use, you may need to add more or less liquid to get the right consistency.

Rolled, layered, filled, folded... we make blini sweet and savoury, thin and thick and use them in starters, mains or desserts. For breakfast they are often enjoyed with tvorog and a warm fruit sauce. Thick blini are dipped into stews like *Mačanka* (see page 132), whereas the more typical thinner ones are rolled around fillings like slow-cooked meat, mushrooms or tvorog (Curd Cheese, see page 81), or served with cured fish and salmon roe. They are also made thin and cooked super-delicately to layer up with buttery poppyseed paste. The recipe opposite uses ghee to fry the blini, but if you prefer you can use salo (Cured Pork Fat, see page 82), as my mum always does.

Blinchiki, blini (*mlyntsi* in Ukrainian, *bliny* in Belarusian) are some of the names for Eastern European pancakes. I use the words blini and blinchiki throughout the book:

• Blini is the name for pancakes served on the side of a dish like a stew or as a base for something, say cured fish.

• Blinchiki is usually used to describe pancakes filled with something and then rolled. The word also translates as 'little blini'.

SERVES 4–6 (MAKES ABOUT 16–18)

350ml (12fl oz) milk
300ml (10½fl oz) water
½ tsp bicarbonate of soda (baking soda)
1 tsp apple cider vinegar
2 eggs
400g (14oz) plain (all-purpose)
  or other flour
generous pinch of salt
1 tsp sugar (optional)
ghee, for frying
butter, for topping

Mix the milk and water in a jug. Stir the bicarbonate of soda and vinegar together in a small cup until it fizzes, then pour into the milk mixture. Break the eggs into a large mixing bowl and whisk thoroughly. Add a quarter of the flour into the bowl with a splash of the liquid. Use a whisk to combine thoroughly into a thickish paste. Add the salt and sugar (if using) and whisk well. Continue adding a quarter of the flour at a time and a splash of the liquid, whisking well before adding the next batch. This will help avoid lumps forming.

Once all the liquid and flour has been added, check the consistency by scooping up a ladleful of the batter and pouring it back into the bowl. It should be silky smooth with a bit of weight and density but not be too thick. Add more milk or water if you feel it needs it. Let the batter stand for 10 minutes.

To cook the blini, heat a 22cm (8in) frying pan over a medium–high heat and add a tablespoon of ghee. Let it melt and coat the whole surface. Give the batter a final whisk, lift up the pan and pour in about three-quarters of a ladleful into the pan, tilting it swiftly so that the batter completely coats the base of the pan. Place back on the heat and cook for a couple of minutes before flipping it over, adding more ghee (I lift one edge slightly and let the extra ghee melt on the pan). Cook until golden on both sides, then transfer to a warm plate. Top with butter, spreading it with a knife over the blini. Repeat with the remaining batter to make about 16 blini, adding ghee to the pan and butter to each cooked blini as you layer them onto the plate.

Blinchiki with Tvorog and Plum Sauce

Blinchiki s tvorogom i slivovym varen'yem

Blinchiki are a breakfast staple and I love to pair them with a jammy plum sauce – this quick version reminds me of my parents making at least 20 jars of plum jam at the end of summer. Select very ripe plums because their natural sugar content is high and their flavour at its best. Make these using my mum's traditional blini batter, exactly the way she cooks them.

SERVES 4–6 (MAKES ABOUT 16–18)

1 x quantity Eastern European Pancakes batter (page 21)
500g (1lb 2oz) tvorog or cottage cheese
soured cream, to serve

For the sauce
6 ripe plums, quartered and stoned
100g (3½oz) raw cane (brown) sugar

First make the sauce. Put the plums and sugar into a deep-sided pan, toss the sugar through the plums and let them stand for 10 minutes, stirring occasionally (this helps release the juice). Place over a medium–high heat and bring to a simmer. Allow to simmer, uncovered, adjusting the heat as necessary, for 15–20 minutes, stirring occasionally. Once the plums have broken down but still have some shape, remove from the heat and set aside until ready to serve, or cool and store in a sterilized jar in the refrigerator.

Alternatively, you could roast the stoned plums, sprinkled with the sugar, at 180°C fan/200°C/400°F/Gas mark 6 for 20–30 minutes.

Meanwhile make 16–18 blinchiki following the instructions on page 21.

To serve, spread a heaped tablespoon of tvorog over the blinchiki and top with a little of the sauce. Fold the blinchiki in half and then in half again. Enjoy while they are freshly made, with a bit of soured cream if you wish.

Mornings

Ukrainian Savoury Toast with Cheese

Hrinky z syrom

This was one of the first meals we ate when we moved to Australia and one my family continues to make. I often walk into my parents' house and know immediately from the tempting smell that Dad is cooking hrinky. They're quickly made with easily sourced ingredients. Use any bread with a bit of texture, especially if it's a few days old: we love sourdough. Hrinky can be made without the egg and cheese, using rye bread simply fried in butter and topped with salted or smoked fish for dinner or lunch. For more of a breakfast spread, serve with seasoned cucumbers, tomato wedges, spring onions and salami.

SERVES 2

2 eggs
125ml (4fl oz) milk
4 thickly cut slices of bread
60g (2¼oz) butter
40g (1½oz) cheddar or other melting
  cheese, sliced thinly
salt and pepper

Whisk the eggs and milk together in a shallow bowl, seasoning with salt and pepper. Dip the bread in the mix, coating the slices on both sides. Heat a large cast-iron pan and, depending on its size, add half the butter and fry two dipped bread slices at a time, for 2 minutes until the underside is golden and crispy. Flip them over and top with a slice of cheese, reduce the heat to medium and cook for 2–3 minutes or until the cheese has melted. Repeat with the remaining butter, bread and cheese.

Serve hot from the pan. Enjoy with hot black coffee.

Fried Eggs in Bread with Vegetables

Glazun'ya v khlebe

This couldn't be easier and it's really quick to put together in one pan. Serve with a platter of freshly sliced vegetables and herbs, such as radishes, spring onions, cucumbers, dill or parsley, seasoning them really well with salt. Just be prepared to have extra ingredients on hand as you might want more!

SERVES 2

2 square- or oval-shaped slices of bread
  – country loaf or sourdough is fine
30g (1oz) butter
2 eggs
salt and pepper
seasoned vegetables and herbs,
  to serve

Cut out the centre of the bread slices about 1–2cm (½–¾in) from the crust, and reserve. Heat a large frying pan over a medium–high heat. Melt the butter, then add all the bread pieces. Fry for 2 minutes or until the underside is golden and crispy. Flip the pieces and carefully add 1 egg to the centre of each cut-out slice. Reduce the heat to medium. Season with salt and pepper and cook for 4–5 minutes until the whites are cooked through, adjusting the heat if needed.

Serve with the extra bread pieces to dip into the yolks, and with crunchy vegetables on the side.

Tvorog and Semolina Bake with Apricot Sauce

Zapekanka s abrikosami

Tvorozhnaya zapekanka is a typical Eastern European curd cheese and semolina bake. It's often served for breakfast but can easily be transformed into a dessert with extra sugar. This one is flavoured with orange zest and sultanas. We often use semolina in breakfast porridge, but here it's used to give this bake some structure yet still keep it light.

SERVES 6–8

butter or oil, for greasing
4 Tbsp semolina (cream of wheat),
   plus extra for dusting
1kg (2lb 4oz) tvorog or cottage cheese;
   opt for a dry style or strain off any
   excess whey
2 eggs
1 heaped Tbsp sugar
70g (2½oz) sultanas (golden raisins)
zest of 1 orange
1 tsp bicarbonate of soda (baking soda)
1 tsp apple cider vinegar
2 Tbsp soured cream, plus extra to serve

For the sauce
6 ripe pitted apricots, cut into wedges
50g (1¾oz) sugar

Preheat the oven to 180°C fan/200°C/400°F/Gas mark 6. Generously grease a 23cm (9in) diameter cake tin or medium rectangular baking tray, then dust the base and sides with a little semolina.

In a medium bowl, mix together the tvorog, eggs, sugar, semolina, sultanas and the orange zest using a fork. In a small separate bowl combine the bicarbonate of soda and vinegar until fizzing, then pour into the cheese mixture. Use the fork to combine and fluff up the mixture a bit.

Transfer the mixture to the prepared tin and spread out evenly, levelling the surface but not pressing down too much. Spread the soured cream over the surface and transfer to the oven. Cook for 50 minutes–1 hour until risen with a darkened or golden surface.

Meanwhile, make the sauce. Put the apricots into a deep-sided saucepan with the sugar and a splash of water over a medium heat. Bring to a simmer, stirring occasionally, and cook for 20–30 minutes or until the apricots have softened, broken down and formed a loose-textured sauce.

Once the zapekanka is ready, remove from the oven and allow to cool for 5 minutes. It will naturally drop a little. Serve warm, with extra soured cream and the apricot sauce.

Mornings

Soft Cheese Pancakes with Mixed Berry Sauce

Syrnyky z yahodamy

Syr is the Ukrainian word for cheese and this is another recipe that uses tvorog. Syrnyky are staple breakfast fare throughout Eastern Europe but can be eaten any time of day. Traditionally, these little pancakes were made as a way of using up surplus tvorog. Try to find a dry-style tvorog, otherwise strain off the whey by placing the cheese in a muslin/cheesecloth-lined sieve over a bowl. Blackcurrant or other berry sauce is just heavenly with these, and a generous amount of soured cream is essential.

SERVES 4 (MAKES 12)

500g (1lb 2oz) tvorog or cottage cheese
1 egg
2 Tbsp sugar, or to taste; you may
  prefer a little extra
2 Tbsp plain (all-purpose) flour,
  plus extra as needed
small pinch of fine salt
butter, for frying
soured cream, to serve

For the sauce
250g (9oz) mixed berries
  (frozen or fresh)
2 heaped Tbsp honey

In a bowl mix the tvorog, egg, sugar, flour and salt using a fork to combine and mash everything together. Add a little extra flour if the mixture is sticky – it needs to be soft and pliable. Use a spoon to scoop about 50g (1¾oz) mounds of the mixture into round thick discs, about 1.5cm thick (¾in). Coat each disc in some extra flour before setting them on a floured board.

Heat some butter in a frying pan and cook the syrnyky in batches over a medium heat for 3–4 minutes each side, adding more butter as needed. Transfer them to a plate lined with paper towel while you cook the rest. Keep warm.

To make the sauce put the berries and the honey in a saucepan over a medium heat and cook at a slight simmer for 7 minutes. Serve the warm syrnyky with the sauce and a big dollop of soured cream.

Buckwheat and Mushroom Porridge

Kasha s gribami

Buckwheat kasha is something Mum would often make. It could be as simple as some freshly cooked toasted buckwheat groats, sprinkled with salt and topped with a generous piece of butter to melt through. Or, for cold autumn or winter mornings, buckwheat is perfect as a savoury porridge with a creamy mushroom sauce. I recommend using toasted buckwheat, which you can buy in Eastern European stores; raw dried buckwheat isn't the same. Make a large batch of this kasha and store it in a jar in the refrigerator to use for salads, too.

SERVES 4

200g (7oz) toasted buckwheat (kasha), rinsed and drained
15g (½oz) butter

For the sauce
20g (¾oz) butter or ghee
½ onion, diced
800g (1lb 12oz) mushrooms (any, or a mix of your choice), cleaned and thinly sliced
1 large garlic clove, crushed
125ml (4fl oz) single (light) cream
small bunches of parsley and dill, roughly chopped
salt and pepper

Put the buckwheat in a medium saucepan and cover with twice the amount of water. Place over a medium–high heat, cover with a lid and bring to the boil. Boil for 30 seconds, then strain through a sieve, discarding the water. Return the buckwheat to the pan, add 500ml (17fl oz) of fresh water and season with salt. Re-cover the pan and return to the lowest heat to simmer for 15–20 minutes or until the buckwheat has entirely absorbed the water. Remove from the heat, add the butter and fluff up the buckwheat using a fork. Put the lid back on and set aside while you make the sauce.

Melt the butter in a large pan over a medium–high heat. Add the onion and cook, stirring occasionally, for 5 minutes. Add the mushrooms and continue to cook for 15 minutes, stirring occasionally, until they have cooked down, stopped releasing water and are golden in colour. Add the garlic, cream, salt and pepper and cook, stirring occasionally, for a further 5 minutes – adjust the heat as needed. Turn off the heat and stir through the chopped herbs. Taste and adjust the seasoning. Serve the buckwheat warm topped with the creamy mushroom sauce.

Buckwheat Pancakes, Two Ways

Grechnevyye oladya

The kitchen of my mum's childhood home in Baranavichy was tiny. Yet, it was always so alive and full of chatter as we gathered, drawn by the sound of butter sizzling on a cast-iron pan and the sight of a bowl of vibrant red strawberries, fresh from the market, on the table. My babushka Lida would be standing at the hob making a pile of her thick, plump oladya. The recipe here is for buckwheat pancakes; although, we use whatever flour is in the cupboard. Buckwheat flour is quite dense so adjust the amount of milk depending on how thick you like your pancakes.

I couldn't decide which flavours I loved more, so here I've included two variations. Or you could serve them like babushka Lida would – with strawberries and soured cream.

SERVES 4

260g (9¼oz) thick, full-fat yoghurt
250ml (9fl oz) milk
1 egg
1 generous Tbsp runny honey,
     plus extra to serve
½ tsp bicarbonate of soda (baking soda)
1 tsp apple cider vinegar
300g (10½oz) buckwheat flour
pinch of salt
butter or oil, for frying
soured cream, to serve

In a large mixing bowl whisk together the yoghurt, milk, egg and honey. Stir the bicarbonate of soda and the vinegar in a small cup until fizzing, then add to the mixing bowl with the flour and salt. Whisk to combine, then let stand for 10 minutes. Give it a final whisk: the batter should be fairly thick but runny.

Heat a large frying pan over a medium–high heat. Add a knob of butter and move it around to coat the surface of the pan as it melts. Add a heaped tablespoon of the batter to the pan for each pancake: you should be able to cook 3–4 simultaneously. Cook for 3 minutes on each side; add more butter for each batch and adjust the heat if it's too high. Serve with soured cream and an extra drizzle of honey, if you like.

VARIATION: BLUEBERRY SAUCE

280g (10oz) blueberries or wild
     blueberries (fresh or frozen)
2 heaped Tbsp runny honey,
     plus extra to serve

Cook the buckwheat pancakes as above. Meanwhile, make the sauce: place the blueberries and honey in a saucepan, bring to a simmer and cook the berries, stirring occasionally, over a medium heat for 5–7 minutes. Serve the sauce warm over the pancakes, with soured cream and an extra drizzle of honey.

Mornings

VARIATION: APPLE AND CINNAMON
1 tsp ground cinnamon
2–3 apples, halved, cored and
   thinly sliced
runny honey, to serve

Prepare the pancakes as opposite, but stir the cinnamon into the pancake batter along with the salt. Leave to stand.

As you add heaped tablespoons of batter into the hot pan, place a few of the apple slices, slightly overlapping, on each pancake. Cook over a medium–high heat for 3 minutes, then flip onto the other side, adding more butter to the pan, reduce the heat to medium and cook for 4 minutes – the apple side will need slightly longer for the batter to cook through completely. Cook the remaining pancakes, adding more butter for each batch.

Serve with a dollop of soured cream and a generous drizzle of runny honey.

From the Garden

From the Garden

Recipes for the growing season

Every year, spring signifies a new start. During this time, people in Ukraine and Belarus begin to set up their *rassada* (the process of growing plants from seeds). City apartment balconies and wide window sills are transformed into growing spaces where seeds are planted into small boxes. Once the seedlings are strong enough, some families transfer them to dachas outside the cities. These simple wooden houses on a plot of land are usually where people spend their weekends, sometimes the entire summer; many are surrounded by forests where more food can be foraged.

Both my families in Belarus and Ukraine had a dacha where they grew vegetables, herbs and greens, fruit trees and bushes, and both were built from scratch. Happily, my mum's family's house is still there and, growing up, we spent summers there when we could.

These gardens shaped much of the vegetable dishes that my family cook and their methods for cooking the vegetables. Often, the dishes are not complicated, but celebrate the seasons. Among my favourites are the Cold Beetroot Borsch (page 38), the simple Cabbage and Cranberry Slaw (page 40), and the Fresh Tomato Salad topped with golden unrefined sunflower oil (page 48).

Cold Beetroot Borsch
Kholodnyk

Kholod means cold, and this soup is called kholodnyk in Ukrainian. It's ideally made and eaten in the height of summer on really hot days when you don't want to cook much. It is vibrant, bright, and the dill will scent your home for hours. Tear up larger beetroot leaves and cook them in the liquid for the last 20 minutes or thinly slice young leaves to serve with the greens. Start this recipe a few hours before serving so that the beetroot liquid has enough time to chill in the refrigerator.

SERVES 4

5 medium–large beetroots (stems and leaves removed, but keep the skin and the natural ends for flavour and colour), washed well
1 tsp apple cider vinegar
4 eggs
2 cucumbers
small bunch of dill
a few stems of spring onions (scallions)
lemon wedges, for squeezing
soured cream, to serve

Put the beetroots in a large saucepan and cover with enough of the measured water to cover the beets and fill the pan three-quarters full, about 2.5 litres (88fl oz). Add the vinegar, cover with a lid and bring to the boil, then reduce the heat and simmer for 1 hour or until the beetroot is cooked through. (Check by piercing one with a fork or skewer: it should easily pass through to the centre.)

Transfer the cooked beets to a bowl, reserving the liquid as this will be the base of the soup. Cool the liquid to room temperature, then transfer the liquid and bowl of beets to the refrigerator for a couple of hours until cold.

Meanwhile, place the eggs in a small saucepan of cold water. Bring to the boil and cook for 9 minutes, then plunge into cold water to stop the cooking. Peel and slice into halves or quarters.

When you are ready to serve, prepare the rest of the ingredients: dice the cucumbers, finely chop the dill, and slice the spring onions. Peel and grate the chilled beetroot.

Divide everything between serving bowls and serve with a squeeze of lemon, a dollop of soured cream and some fresh bread, if you like.

From the Garden

Cabbage and Cranberry Slaw

Salata z kapusty i žuraviny

On chilly autumn mornings my mum used to be taken by her dad to forage for wild cranberries in the region outside their town in western Belarus. She still talks about how she disliked foraging for frost-covered cranberries, unlike other wild foods, which were easier and more pleasant to gather. Despite Mum's dislike of those early-morning tramps over swampy wet ground, her love of cranberries is evident. This slaw is a great base for them: the combination of juices from the cranberries, cabbage and other ingredients works well. Allowing it to stand once everything is combined seems to go against all soggy-salad rules, but it's delicious, as the released juices create a sort of fast ferment flavour.

SERVES 4–6 AS A SIDE

400g (14oz) red cabbage (about a
    quarter of a cabbage, stem removed),
    thinly shredded
1 carrot, grated
½ beetroot, grated
1 green apple, cored and grated
small handful of cranberries or
    lingonberries (if frozen defrost at room
    temperature for a couple of hours)
1 Tbsp apple cider vinegar
juice of ½ lemon
1 Tbsp honey
salt

Put the shredded cabbage in a large mixing bowl, add 2 pinches of salt and massage the cabbage using your hands for 2 minutes. The salt will help release the juices. Add the grated carrot, beetroot and apple along with the cranberries and roughly combine.

In a separate bowl, stir the vinegar, lemon juice and honey together. Pour over the salad and mix well. Leave it to stand for 1 hour until the ingredients have softened slightly and released liquid. Unless serving immediately, cover and place in the refrigerator.

When ready to serve, mix the slaw once more and taste again now that the flavours have developed. Season with salt if needed.

From the Garden

Barley Pilaf with Plums and Walnut Pesto

Piarloŭki sa slivami i hreckimi arechami

My babushka Lida would grow plenty of green herbs in her garden including copious amounts of parsley, dill and even basil. There is also a plum tree growing in front of her dacha. Throughout the summer we often make pestos to serve with pearl barley and other grains, even buckwheat noodles. The earthy pearl barley, sweet and sour plums and mushrooms are a great combination with sweet roasted onions and fresh pesto. This and the cucumber salad (page 44) would be lovely served as sides to the Lamb Skewers (page 108) or the Stuffed Chicken Rissoles (page 168).

SERVES 4 AS A SIDE

200g (7oz) pearl barley, rinsed
200g (7oz) chestnut (Swiss) mushrooms or other seasonal ones, cleaned then halved or quartered
4 plums, halved and pitted
1 red (bell) pepper, deseeded and cut into wedges
2 onions or shallots, quartered
30g (1oz) butter, melted
salt and pepper

For the pesto
50g (1¾oz) walnuts
½ bunch of parsley
½ bunch of dill
½ bunch of basil
1 garlic clove
generous drizzle of golden unrefined sunflower oil

Put the pearl barley in a saucepan with 750ml (26fl oz) water. Add a pinch of salt and bring to the boil. Cover with a lid and lower the heat to simmer for 25–30 minutes, stirring occasionally, or until all the water has been absorbed. You may need to add more water. Once cooked, transfer to a large bowl and leave to cool, stirring occasionally.

Preheat the oven to 180°C fan/200°C/400°F/Gas mark 6. Spread the mushrooms, plums and the vegetables over a baking tray, drizzle with the butter and season with salt and pepper. Roast for 30 minutes.

To make the pesto, soak the walnuts in a small bowl of water for 15 minutes. Drain, then add to a blender with the herbs, garlic and oil. Blend and season with salt to taste.

Stir a spoonful of the pesto through the pearl barley, then toss through the roasted mushrooms, plums and veg, along with any juices in the tray. Serve warm or cool with extra pesto on the side.

From the Garden

Express Cucumber, Honey and Dill Salad

Salata z ahurkami

This vibrant, tangy salad comes together quickly and effortlessly. You do need to season the cucumbers with salt 10 minutes before serving so that they release juice for the dressing. I recommend having this as a savoury refresher with one of the breakfast dishes, like Ukrainian Savoury Toast (page 25) or Fried Eggs in Bread (page 26). It also pairs nicely with the Stuffed Chicken Rissoles (page 168) and boiled potatoes.

SERVES 4 AS A SIDE

3 cucumbers (preferably cold
   from the refrigerator)
salt
½ small bunch of dill, roughly chopped,
   thick stems removed
generous glug of golden unrefined
   sunflower oil, plus an extra
   drizzle to serve
1 heaped tsp runny honey
2 Tbsp apple cider vinegar
sea salt flakes (optional)

Quarter the cucumbers lengthways then in half (or keep them long). Place in a bowl and season with a generous pinch of salt. Set aside for 10 minutes, turning them once or twice. Add the dill to the bowl.

In a separate small bowl thoroughly combine the oil, honey and vinegar. Pour over the cucumbers, tossing the ingredients with the dressing to coat the cucumbers well. Transfer to a plate, drizzle extra oil on top and some flaky sea salt, if you like. Serve fresh.

From the Garden

Summer Garden Salad
Letniy salat

This might look like a simple salad, but something incredible happens when you add soured cream to it all. The natural juices from the vegetables create a beautiful dressing for all the ingredients. You can also scoop this salad onto rye bread, and pour a spoonful of the dressing over the lot. It may seem like a lot of soured cream, but it's what makes this salad so special.

SERVES 4–6 AS A SIDE

3 tomatoes (preferably heirloom
   tomatoes) cut into wedges
1 large cucumber, halved lengthways
   and finely sliced
¼ bunch of spring onions (scallions) or
   ½ red onion, roughly chopped
4 radishes, halved and thinly sliced
¼ bunch of dill, roughly chopped
handful of salad leaves
good drizzle of golden unrefined
   sunflower oil
about 125ml (4fl oz) soured cream
   (adjust to your liking)
salt and pepper

Add all the vegetables and herbs to a large bowl and add generous amounts of salt, pepper and oil. Add the soured cream and toss the ingredients well, coating everything in the cream. Leave to stand for a few minutes before serving.

Fresh Tomato Salad
Salat z pomidoriv

Something I am reminded of time and time again is that when the ingredients are good, you don't need to do much to them – as with this fresh tomato salad. Pour unrefined sunflower oil over these salted tomatoes and it smells as if you have just toasted fresh sunflower seeds in your pan. You can find high-quality unrefined sunflower oil at a stockist I recommend on page 201.

SERVES 4-6 AS A SIDE

small handful of lettuce leaves or young
   beetroot leaves, or other salad greens,
   washed and dried
6–7 heirloom tomatoes (assorted
   varieties and colours), very
   thinly sliced
½ small red onion, thinly sliced
½ red chilli, thinly sliced (optional)
small handful of dill, fronds torn
golden unrefined sunflower oil
sea salt flakes
fresh bread, to serve (optional)

Tear the lettuce leaves slightly and arrange them on a plate. Top with the tomatoes, overlapping the slices, then add the sliced onion. Season very generously with sea salt flakes and leave to stand for 5 minutes and release the juice. Top with the chilli, dill, a very generous glug of sunflower oil and an extra pinch of salt. Serve this with bread to mop up the juice.

From the Garden

Herby Potato Salad

Kartoplyanny salat z zelennyu

My parents often serve boiled potatoes fresh from the garden with slabs of butter, a jar of salt and a platter of the freshest herbs and it's one of my favourite things to eat, like this recipe. Small young potatoes work best for a cold salad, although feel free to use any seasonal potatoes – chop large ones into smaller pieces. Add lots of salt and pepper, as I find potatoes often need it. Make this at least 2 hours ahead of serving.

SERVES 4–6 AS A SIDE

1kg (2lb 4oz) small to medium potatoes,
   scrubbed clean
½ bunch of spring onions (scallions)
½ bunch of dill
½ bunch of parsley
1 large cucumber

For the dressing
200ml (7fl oz) soured cream
1 heaped tsp Dijon mustard
zest and juice of 1 lemon
salt and pepper
golden unrefined sunflower oil

Put the unpeeled potatoes in a large pan and fill with water. Add a generous amount of salt and cover with a lid. Bring to a simmer and cook for 12–15 minutes, depending on the type and size of potato. Check that they are cooked by piercing one of the potatoes with a fork – it's ready when the centre feels soft. Drain, and let the potatoes cool to room temperature. Peel and discard the skins and chop the potatoes into quarters. Transfer to a bowl, cover with a plate or cling film (plastic wrap) and place in the refrigerator for at least 45 minutes.

Prepare the rest of the ingredients and make the dressing 15 minutes before you want to serve. Finely chop the spring onions, dill and parsley (removing any ends and stems). Halve the cucumber lengthways, then slice into half-moons, not too thin.

Mix together the soured cream, mustard, lemon zest and juice, some salt and pepper and a generous glug of oil in a small bowl. Taste and adjust the seasoning.

In a large mixing bowl combine the potatoes with the dressing, cucumbers and chopped herbs. Mix well. Taste and add more seasoning, herbs, lemon or soured cream as you prefer!

From the Garden

From the Garden

Whipped Herby Tvorog with Courgettes

Zharenyye kabachki s tvorogom

Seasoned well and with a drizzle of oil, tvorog makes a beautiful base for this recipe. A little soured cream lends the tvorog extra creaminess. This is a great one for sharing, or serving as a side to a main dish. If you want to use aubergine instead of courgettes, or even some ripe raw or slow-roasted tomatoes, they are equally delicious. I use 'grey' courgettes, which are the light green variety.

SERVES 4–6

3 medium courgettes (zucchini), thinly
    sliced into rounds (about 5mm/¼in)
5 Tbsp plain (all-purpose) flour
butter or oil, for frying
1 garlic clove, crushed
flatbreads, to serve
salt

For the whipped tvorog
500g (1lb 2oz) tvorog or cottage cheese
2 Tbsp soured cream
juice of 1 lemon
½ bunch of fresh dill, finely chopped
golden unrefined sunflower oil,
    for drizzling

Spread the courgette slices on a tray, then sprinkle all over with salt. Liquid will start to form. Tip the slices into a bowl with the flour and toss to cover lightly.

Heat a large frying pan and add the butter or oil. Cook the courgette slices in batches, over a medium–high heat, until golden and slightly crisp. Sprinkle with more salt on each side as you cook them and add more butter or oil as needed. Set aside on a plate lined with paper towels.

In a separate bowl, mix together the tvorog, soured cream, lemon juice, dill and a drizzle of sunflower oil. Season generously with salt. Spread out this mixture on a plate or platter. Top with the courgettes, the crushed garlic and an extra generous drizzle of oil. Enjoy with flatbreads or other bread for dipping.

Potato Pancakes
Dranyky

Dranyky (also known as *deruny* in Ukrainian) are one of the national dishes of Belarus – these delicious potato pancakes have a crisp golden surface and soft inside; they pair perfectly with soured cream. You can use old potatoes for these pancakes, as my babushka Lida often would. The potatoes she grew and harvested in Belarus were stored in large bags that ensured they would last for months. She'd use them for various dishes over the coming year, even as fresher potatoes became available at the markets – as a result of living through hard times, she was accustomed to avoiding waste. Grating potatoes by hand takes a while, although it's perfectly possible. If you have the option, use a food processor.

SERVES 4 (MAKES 12)

1kg (2lb 4oz) potatoes, peeled
1 egg
2–3 Tbsp plain (all-purpose) flour
salt
butter, ghee or oil, for cooking
soured cream, to serve

Coarsely grate the potatoes and add to a large bowl with the egg, flour and a few large pinches of salt. Mix everything together well.

Heat a frying pan to a high heat. Add a generous amount of butter and tilt the pan to spread it over the base. Add a large heaped tablespoon of the potato mixture to the sizzling-hot pan and flatten into a thin disc, about 2mm (1/16in). Reduce the heat slightly if you find it's too hot for the pancakes. You should be able to cook about four at a time, depending on the size of your pan, adding more butter when you flip them to the other side. Cook for 3–4 minutes on each side or until the surface is golden and the centre cooked right through. Adjust the heat accordingly – you'll get a feel for the best temperature after the first couple. Keep scooping and stirring the potato liquid through the mixture as it helps cook the potato right through without drying out.

Serve immediately, warm from the pan, with soured cream.

From the Garden

Roasted Stuffed Peppers

Perets s syrom iz dukhovki

I love these roasted stuffed peppers as they're so vibrant and versatile.
My aunt, Marina, once made these for me, but instead of slicing them
lengthways, she sliced them into rings and served them drizzled with oil
– you can prepare them as you like. Bryndza is an Eastern European sheep's
milk cheese very similar to feta – you can also throw that in too. If your
tvorog is runny, place it in a muslin/cheesecloth-lined sieve and squeeze out
any excess liquid. Add as many herbs as you like.

SERVES 4–6

100g (3½oz) havarti or other melting
   cheese such as a light cheddar, firm
   mozzarella or sulguni, grated
500g (1lb 2oz) tvorog or cottage cheese;
   or add some bryndza to the mix
2 Tbsp soured cream
handful each of dill, parsley, spring
   onions (scallions), roughly chopped
6 long red (bell) peppers, sliced
   lengthways, stems on but
   seeds removed
golden unrefined sunflower oil,
   for drizzling
salt

Preheat the oven to 180°C fan/200°C/400°F/Gas mark 6.
Weigh and set aside 40g (1½oz) of the havarti. Mix the rest of
the cheese with the tvorog, soured cream, herbs and some
salt to taste in a bowl. Fill the pepper halves with the cheese
and herb filling, then top each one with the rest of the grated
havarti. Place on a baking tray lined with baking paper. Drizzle
with oil and sprinkle with extra salt. Roast in the oven for
30–40 minutes or until the peppers have softened and the
tops are golden. Serve warm.

From the Garden

Courgette, Pumpkin and Carrot Pancakes

Ovoshchnyye oladya

We call these pancakes rather than fritters because they are less dried out from the frying process than fritters – the liquid from the vegetables is retained and helps to soften and steam the pancakes as they cook, meaning the outside encases all the beautiful flavours, sweetness and texture of the vegetables.

SERVES 4 (MAKES 12)

120g (4¼oz) pumpkin (1 small wedge), peeled
2 medium courgettes (zucchini)
1 large carrot
small handful of dill fronds, finely chopped
2 eggs
3 Tbsp plain (all-purpose) flour
salt and pepper to taste
butter, ghee or oil, for cooking
soured cream, crème fraîche or yoghurt, to serve

Coarsely grate all the vegetables and add to a large bowl with the dill, eggs and flour. Season with salt and pepper and mix thoroughly together.

Heat a pan to a high heat. Add a knob of butter or drizzle of oil and tilt the pan to spread it over the surface. Reduce to a medium–high heat and scoop a heaped tablespoonful of the vegetable mixture from the bowl into the hot pan. Flatten the mixture down to a thin disc. You should be able to cook about four at a time, depending on the size of your pan, adding more butter when you flip them to the other side. Cook for 2–3 minutes on each side or until the surface is golden and the centre cooked right through. Adjust the heat accordingly – you'll get a feel for the best temperature after the first couple. Taste one to check the seasoning and adjust to your liking. Keep mixing the liquid in the bowl as you scoop each tablespoonful.

Serve immediately, warm from the pan, while the surface of the fritters is still crispy and the centre soft. Enjoy with soured cream, crème fraîche or yoghurt.

Preservation

Preservation

Recipes for ferments, preserves & pickles

Most apartment buildings in Ukraine and Belarus have a lower-ground or underground communal space for storage, which residents usually turn into shelving with endless rows of jars of ferments, sweet and sour preserves and pickles. Each jar has a story, whether it was filled with locally grown and harvested produce from a family's dacha, or foraged from forests or wild spaces. Likewise, many traditional village houses have an 'earth refrigerator' underground, accessed by ladder. Before electric refrigerators and freezers were commonplace in homes, people relied on age-old ways to preserve the glut of the growing season for use during the long cold months when little food was locally available, adding colour and flavour to the standard winter produce. Anything that wasn't eaten immediately would be dried, cured, fermented, cooked in sugar or steeped in alcohol.

Preserving can be done, with or without heat, using sugar to turn fruits into jams, or salt to create ferments. Acid can create a pickle, and the addition of bacterial cultures to milk can transform it into kefir and tvorog.

Homemade preserves really extend your meal options. A large batch of sauerkraut keeps in the refrigerator ready for use as a side if you don't have fresh vegetables to hand. It can then be added to salads, or cooked with plain cabbage for extra flavour. Cucumbers and tomatoes can be fermented or pickled to enjoy along with cheese or main dishes – a simple way to include flavoursome veg in your diet throughout the year.

The basics for pickling and fermentation

- For preserving, use sterilized air-tight jars with lids.

- Sterilize your jars and lids to reduce the chance of mould or unwanted bacteria developing. To sterilize, place the washed jars (rubber seals and lids removed) in a large saucepan over a medium heat, cover with water and bring to the boil. Leave for 10 minutes before removing carefully with tongs and placing on kitchen towel to dry. In a separate pan, do the same for the rubber seals and lids.

- Keep any bowls or jars that are fermenting away from any direct sunlight.

- Adjust your jar size according to your needs. I give a guide, but use smaller or larger jars if that suits you. Once opened, store pickles and ferments in the refrigerator, where they will continue to ferment, but much slower.

- Traditionally preserves were made to last for a whole year – until the next growing season. This requires their sugar content to be very high. The recipes I'm sharing are for everyday eating, so I've reduced the amount of sugar in all jams and preserves. Even with the reduced sugar they will keep for a good few months in the refrigerator.

- Preserving is best done with the freshest ingredients you can find. Fresh, ripe produce lasts longer once preserved and makes for better flavours in brines and syrups.

Sauerkraut with Apple

Kvašanaja kapusta z jablykam

Making sauerkraut always takes me back to my mum's kitchen, where the bench would disappear under a mound of shredded cabbage. This recipe makes a crunchy-style sauerkraut which, freshly fermented, is good to eat after about five days. With more time it continues to evolve slowly, even in the refrigerator, changing colour and texture as it ages. Once it's much older we tend to cook with it, mixing it with fresh cabbage for added tang, and we use it for fried or baked hand pies, stews, pancakes and much more.

A pre-cut cabbage won't work as well here because the amount of liquid in the leaves will vary. When you select a cabbage at your local shop, ask for a fresh, whole, untrimmed one – it will make a better brine. Any excess brine can be saved and used in soups and stews. Start with a bit less salt if using a small cabbage – you can always add more later if it needs extra seasoning.

MAKES ABOUT 4 x 1-LITRE (35FL OZ) JARS

1 whole large green cabbage
2 carrots, coarsely grated
40–50g (1¾oz) sea salt flakes
1–2 green apples or, for something a little different, try 150g (5½oz) cranberries instead of the apple

Peel away the first few dark-green cabbage leaves and set aside. Give the cabbage a rinse and cut into quarters or smaller chunks. Shred the cabbage using a mandoline or in a food processor, discarding the stem.

Transfer the shredded cabbage to an extra-large bowl. Top with the grated carrot and sprinkle with the salt. Use your hands to crush and massage the cabbage and carrot with the salt, rubbing the cabbage to help release its juices. Keep working it for 10–15 minutes – it will start to decrease in volume, and juice will form around the edges and in the bowl: this becomes the brine for fermenting the cabbage mix. Use your hands to distribute the brine.

Once the cabbage mixture is ready, core and slice the apples into thin wedges and toss them through. Place the mixture along with the juices into a separate large bowl suitable for fermenting (glass, ceramic or enamel). Push the mixture down with your hands, pressing heavily so that the juice rises. Top with the reserved cabbage leaves (tear them into smaller

pieces, if necessary) and then place a plate over the lot. Set a heavy object on top to weigh the plate and cabbage mix down; you should see some of the brine coming up to the surface. Push down further if you need to get more of the brine rising to the surface: you need to ensure the cabbage is fully submerged. Cover with a light kitchen cloth or muslin cloth (cheesecloth) and tie securely around the sides. Set aside on the worktop, away from direct sunlight, to ferment for 3 days.

After 3 days, remove the cloth, weight and plate from the bowl. Mix the sauerkraut thoroughly, then leave to breathe, uncovered, for 1 hour. Repeat the process of pressing down on the cabbage, weighting it with a plate and a heavy object, and retie the cloth around the bowl. Let it stand for another 1–2 days (depending on the season it might need longer). Taste after a total of 4–5 days: the mixture should taste salty without any bitterness and it should be crunchy.

Transfer the sauerkraut into sterilized jars along with the brine. Pack tightly and cover the surface with one of the larger torn cabbage leaves. Seal the jars with a lid and place in the refrigerator, where the sauerkraut will last for a couple of months before it loses its crunch.

Preservation

Fermented Dill Cucumbers

Malosolniy ogurzy

Quick-fermented cucumbers are ideal to make during the summer – they can be ready after 1–2 days because of the warmer temperatures. This recipe doesn't use vinegar: the cucumbers are preserved with salt and flavoured with garlic. Try to find gherkin cucumbers or other small varieties. At home, we love to serve a plate of these in the centre of the table as a side to many dishes.

MAKES 2 x 1.5-LITRE (52FL OZ) JARS OR 1 x 3-LITRE (105FL OZ) JAR

1kg (2lb 4oz) gherkin (pickling) cucumbers, washed and ends trimmed
1 bunch of dill, fronds and stems, washed
3 garlic cloves, peeled and halved lengthways
1 heaped tsp whole allspice
1 heaped tsp black peppercorns
1 Tbsp dill seeds
1 large bay leaf
½ tsp mustard seeds
1.5 litres (52fl oz) boiling water
20g (¾oz) salt

First, sterilize your jars, ideally ones with a wide opening (see page 62). Halve any long cucumbers widthways so they can stand upright in the jars.

Place the fresh dill in the bottom of the jar(s) and push it down. Add the garlic, allspice, peppercorns, dill seeds, bay leaf and mustard seeds to your jar(s) and pack in the cucumbers tightly, side by side.

Pour the measured boiling water into a jug, add the salt and stir to dissolve. Pour it into the jar(s), making sure the cucumbers are submerged. Cover with a plate and set aside at room temperature. Leave for 24–48 hours before sealing with a lid and placing in the refrigerator. They are ready to eat straight away – they're gone within a week in my home – but they can last in the refrigerator for a few weeks; the flavour becomes stronger over time.

Tip: If you have dill heads or any sort of berry leaves, such as redcurrants, blackcurrants, raspberries, etc., add them to the jar and the cucumbers will stay crunchier.

Preservation

Pickled Tomatoes
Marynovani pomidory

We use small tomatoes for these pickles – they pop in your mouth as you eat them! They are beautiful as a side dish to the Stuffed Chicken Rissoles (page 168), Lamb Skewers (page 108), Potato Pancakes with Pork Filling (page 143), and practically all other savoury dishes in this book. Try them with a shot of vodka, too – you won't regret it.

MAKES 2 x 1.5-LITRE (52FL OZ) JARS OR SEVERAL SMALLER ONES

1 bunch of dill, fronds and stems, washed
2 bay leaves
5–6 garlic cloves, peeled and halved lengthways
1 heaped tsp whole allspice
1 heaped tsp black peppercorns
1 heaped tsp dill seeds
4–6 small chillies (optional)
1.5kg (3lb 5oz) small tomatoes, washed and dried thoroughly
1.5 litres (52fl oz) boiling water
1 tsp sugar
1 Tbsp salt
1 Tbsp vinegar

First, sterilize your jars (see page 62).

Place half the herbs, garlic, spices, seeds and chillies, if using, in the bottom of the jars. Add the tomatoes and top with the rest of the herbs, garlic and spices.

Pour the measured boiling water into a jug, add the sugar, salt and vinegar, stir to dissolve, then pour into the jars. Seal tightly with the lids and let stand for up to 3 days on the worktop, away from direct sunlight. Transfer to the refrigerator when you notice small bubbles appearing and wait for at least 2 weeks before opening. Once opened they last well in the refrigerator, for a month at least.

Preservation

Preservation

Pickled Cucumbers in Tomato Sauce

Marynovani ohirky v tomatnomu sousi

For this recipe, use gherkin cucumbers if you can – they have a thicker skin so work well for pickling – but smaller cucumbers will be fine, too. Traditionally the tomato sauce is made fresh but I buy rustic-style passata with seeds in. If you can find any, add a fresh dill head, or the leaves of horseradish, cherries or blackcurrants, which help keep the cucumbers crunchy. Once you open a jar, you can add the sauce to soups or even cocktails (see the tip, below).

MAKES 2 x 1.5-LITRE (52FL OZ) JARS

1kg (2lb 4oz) gherkin (pickling) cucumbers (or other small cucumber variety)
350ml (12fl oz) rustic-style passata
800ml (28fl oz) water
1 Tbsp sugar (optional)
20g (¾oz) salt
2 tsp white vinegar
2 large garlic cloves, peeled and halved lengthways
1 tsp whole allspice
1 tsp peppercorns
1 tsp dill seeds
1 large bay leaf
½ bunch of dill

If using gherkin cucumbers, let them soak first in a bowl of cool water for 4 hours. Wash the cucumbers, then trim off the ends. Sterilize your jars (see page 62).

To make the tomato sauce, pour the passata and measured water into a large lidded saucepan. Bring to a simmer, add the sugar and salt and stir to dissolve. Cook for 5 minutes, then turn off the heat and stir through the vinegar. Cover with a lid to keep hot.

Meanwhile, divide the garlic, spices and herbs between the jars. Pack in the cucumbers, arranging them so they stand upright. Check that the tomato sauce is still very hot (bring back to a simmer if it's cooled down) and pour it carefully into the jars. Seal tightly with the lids, turn the jars upside down and cover with a warm towel. Leave until completely cool, then store in the refrigerator. The cucumbers will keep a few weeks once opened.

Tip: Once opened, you can use the tomato sauce for a quick vodka cocktail: add ice, 2 tablespoons vodka and equal amounts or more of the pickled tomato sauce to a cocktail shaker. Shake vigorously and serve cold over ice.

Pickled Beetroots

Marinovannaya svekla

This pickle is beautiful to serve as a side to something like the Roast Duck with Buckwheat (see page 72). The leaves can be finely sliced and added to borsch (see pages 125 and 127), and the stems can simply be snacked on or eaten with some buttered dark rye bread. Use a wide jar if you have one.

MAKES ENOUGH TO FILL A 1-LITRE (35FL OZ) JAR

10–12 small beetroots, including stems and leaves, washed well but unpeeled
3 garlic cloves, halved lengthways
1 long green or red chilli (optional)
1 bay leaf
1 tsp whole allspice
1 tsp black peppercorns
½ bunch each of dill and parsley
800ml (28fl oz) boiling water
2 tsp salt
1 tsp sugar (optional)
1 Tbsp white vinegar

First sterilize your jar (see page 62).

Slice the stems off the beetroots, then cut the leaves off the stems, slicing any long stems in half. Tie the stems together with kitchen string. Set aside, with the leaves.

Place the beetroots in a large lidded saucepan. Pour over enough water to just cover the beetroots. Place the lid on top and bring to the boil. Reduce to a simmer and cook for 30–40 minutes, adding the stems to the pan for the last 3–4 minutes or so. Check one of the larger beetroots is cooked through by piercing to the centre. Once cooked, drain the beetroots and leave them to cool slightly, then peel, keeping them whole.

Place the beetroot leaves in the base of the jar, followed by the garlic, chilli, bay leaf and half the spices and herbs. Arrange the beetroots compactly, tuck the stems into the spaces, and add the remaining spices and herbs on top.

Pour the measured boiling water into a jug, add the salt, sugar and vinegar, then mix to dissolve and pour into the jar. Seal tightly with a lid and turn upside down. Cover with a warm towel and leave to cool completely. Once cool, keep in the refrigerator, where the beetroot will last a few months.

Preservation

Foraging and Preserving Mushrooms

We often end our summers preserving and start our autumns foraging, a tradition my family brought with them from Eastern Europe. Often, autumn in Sydney means it's cold and raining. Just outside the city are a few forests where wild mushrooms grow. We set off early morning, our cars laden with food, hot tea, picnic rugs, extra socks and jumpers, and empty baskets ready to be filled with edible mushrooms. After spending the whole day foraging and cooking up lunch in the forest, we head home for the real work to begin. We only forage once a year, so we try to gather enough mushrooms to last for a while. Once home, we divide mushrooms into piles – for pickling, fermenting, drying and freezing, and some for cooking up fresh. The tables and worktops end up covered with mushrooms of all shapes and sizes. Jars are then sterilized, waiting to be filled. Pots of water are on the boil, ready for mushrooms to be dropped in, their earthy aroma filling the air. I love autumn and the ensuing foraging, connecting me, my friends and family to our continued traditions.

SAFETY NOTE
If you do forage for mushrooms, go with an experienced mushroom forager or join a guided food foraging tour. Never use wild mushrooms unless you know them to be safe.

Preparing

If you're using certain sorts of wild mushrooms, such as chanterelles, first place them in a large bowl of water and leave to soak for a while. The soil will separate from the mushrooms. Repeat this process twice, refilling the bowl with fresh water. Transfer the mushrooms to a tea towel to lightly dry and pat them with another.

Drying

In Eastern Europe, edible mushrooms are foraged in July and August, then dried hanging on strings in a warm, shaded place. The varieties that are especially suitable for drying include porcini, chanterelles and birch bolete. Once dried, mushrooms can be either ground to a powder using a coffee grinder, ready to be added into soups and stews, or stored whole in jars.

To rehydrate whole dried mushrooms, add them to a large bowl and pour over enough boiling water to completely cover the mushrooms. Cover the bowl and leave overnight. The following day, heat them in their soaking water to a simmer, then strain off or reuse that water for soup or stew. Squeeze the water from the mushrooms, before chopping and cooking.

Freezing

Edible wild mushroom varieties can often be found at fresh food markets. If you find yourself drawn to buying a box of these or you have foraged a whole basket of them, they don't last long in the refrigerator, some changing colour almost immediately. It's best to freeze them if you're not pickling or frying them all. Spread them out on trays or boards lined with baking paper that fit your freezer. Freeze for a few hours, then transfer to lidded containers. Use from frozen in soups and stews.

Mushroom Pickles
Marinovannyye griby

If you can't find pine mushrooms for these pickles, white button mushrooms are a good alternative – keep them whole. Serve with thinly sliced raw onion and a shot of vodka for a classic combination.

MAKES 4 JARS (ABOUT 400–500G/ 14–18OZ EACH)

1.5kg (3lb 5oz) pine mushrooms (saffron milk caps), washed or brushed, whole, halved or quartered into similar sizes
20 or so black peppercorns
4 cloves
4 bay leaves
4 garlic cloves, peeled and halved lengthways
8 heaped tsp salt, plus an extra pinch
200ml (7fl oz) vinegar

Three-quarters fill a large saucepan with water and add a generous pinch of salt. Bring to the boil and add the mushrooms. Simmer continuously for 10 minutes over a medium heat.

Meanwhile sterilize your jars (see page 62).

Divide the spices, bay leaves and garlic between the jars. Use a slotted spoon to scoop the boiled mushrooms into a bowl, reserving the cooking water. Divide the mushrooms evenly between the jars. Measure 2 litres (70fl oz) of the cooking water into a large jug. Add the salt and vinegar and stir to dissolve, then pour this liquid into the jars, filling each one to the top (if there isn't enough, add some extra boiling water).

Two-thirds fill a large wide stockpot with water. Place over a medium heat until the water is hot but not boiling. Carefully place the jars in the pot, then cover with their lids but don't seal them tightly yet. Ensure the water is going two-thirds of the way up the outside of jar. Bring to a simmer and cook for 15 minutes. Use heatproof kitchen gloves to transfer the jars carefully from the stockpot to the worktop. Close the lids tightly and carefully turn the jars over. Cover with a warm towel and leave to cool entirely.

Leave the pickles for at least 2 weeks before eating. Unopened, they can be kept for up to a year.

Fermented Pepper Sauce
Adjika

This is my family's version of adjika and we nearly always have a bottle of this ready to throw into soups, stews and sauces for an extra punch of flavour. It pairs really well with the Lamb Skewers (page 108). I also love to add this into pasta and pizza sauces. It lasts for a few months in the refrigerator, thanks to the amount of garlic and salt. If you are not ready to peel 45 garlic cloves, buy them pre-peeled or just make half a batch of this. It might seem like a lot of garlic but its intensity softens once fermented and combined with the sugar from the peppers.

MAKES 4 x 750ML (26FL OZ) BOTTLES

3kg (6lb 8oz) fresh, ripe red (bell) peppers, washed and dried thoroughly
3 large heads of garlic (about 45 cloves)
4–6 chillies
1 large bunch each of coriander (cilantro) and parsley
70g (2½oz) salt

Sterilize your bottles (see page 62).

Halve and deseed the red peppers and place, in batches, in a food processor. Process until finely crushed, transferring each batch to a large bowl. Do the same with the garlic, chillies and herbs. Transfer to the same bowl and add the salt. Mix thoroughly. At this stage it tastes strongly salty, but the flavours will settle and change over the coming days.

Set aside, away from direct sunlight, and cover the bowl with a kitchen cloth. Let stand and ferment for at least 3 days, preferably 5, depending on the weather.

To check the adjika is ready, you will need to taste it: it will have lost its 'raw' flavour, the spices will have mellowed and you should taste the sweetness of the peppers.

When ready, taste, adjust the salt if needed and transfer to your sterilized bottles, then seal with lids and place in the refrigerator. Every day, open the lids to release any pressure that builds up and then re-seal. The sauce continues to ferment in the refrigerator but at a far slower rate.

Preservation

Curd Cheese
Tvorog

Tvorog, *syr* in Ukrainian, is a curd cheese made by heating milk and adding kefir or yoghurt – it is a staple throughout Eastern European cuisines. Many versions are found at markets in Belarus and Ukraine, but it is often made at home using cow's or goat's milk. Nowadays we make our own because it's easy to make and, once ready, it can be used in many ways, as you'll see throughout the book. I also really love it simply as is, topped with some soured cream and mixed berries.

MAKES ABOUT 1KG (2LB 4OZ)

4 litres (140fl oz) full-fat (whole) milk, preferably organic and unhomogenized
500ml (17fl oz) kefir or yoghurt, preferably organic with gut-friendly bacteria (half of each is also fine)

Pour the milk into an extra-large, lidded, ovenproof stockpot and gently heat to 35°C/95°F. Turn off the heat. Stir through the kefir or yoghurt. Cover with a lid and place in a warm spot for 24 hours.

After about 24 hours, when the milk mixture has curdled, preheat the oven to 160°C fan/180°C/350°F/Gas mark 4. Use a knife to score through the curd a few times, in all directions. Cover with a lid and place the pot in the oven for about 20 minutes, then check to see if whey has formed and separated from the curds. Once it has, switch off the oven and leave the tvorog to cool inside, still covered with the lid. It's ready for the next steps when you can see there is a solid cheese mass.

Place the tvorog into the centre of a large piece of muslin cloth (cheesecloth) in a colander over a bowl and leave to drain for around 8 hours. After 8 hours, bring the edges of the cloth together and squeeze it tightly over the bowl (save the whey – it can be stored in a jar in the refrigerator and used in recipes like the Blinchiki on page 22).

Once you've fully squeezed the whey from the tvorog, store it in an airtight container in the refrigerator for up to a week.

Cured Pork Fat
Salo

This cured pork fat can be eaten thinly sliced or used in many of the dishes in this book, such as borsch (page 125) and other soups and stews, potato babka (page 144) and pancakes (page 20). It's common to find different sorts of salo in the markets of Ukraine and Belarus, but many families, including mine, make it at home. When my parents first moved to Australia and salo was not readily available, they would make this recipe. Ask your butcher for a thick piece of pork belly fat with minimal or no meat. Caraway, coriander and dill seeds can all be used, but feel free to add other herbs and spices. Store in the freezer for up to 4 months.

MAKES 1 MEDIUM PIECE

300g (10½oz) pork belly fat (choose a thick fatty piece)
about 80g (2¾oz) sea salt (or other textured salt)
2 large garlic cloves, peeled and sliced lengthways into thirds
2 Tbsp herbs and spices of your choice

Place the pork fat on a medium tray. Pour 50g (1¾oz) of the salt directly onto the fat and coat; entirely cover the surface of the pork fat, patting and pressing the salt to the edges. Press the garlic and herbs and spices onto the surface as well. Cover with a sheet of baking paper and place a heavy object (say, a jar filled with water) on top of it, weighing the pork fat down. Set aside undisturbed for 2 days.

After 2 days, pour away the liquid in the tray and remove the garlic. Dry the pork fat with paper towels and recoat the surface with the remaining salt as you did on day one. Cover again with baking paper and weight it down. Leave for 1 more day.

After 3 days, brush off the excess salt, wrap the salo tightly in baking paper and a plastic bag and store in the freezer.

Preservation

Preservation

Summer Fruit Jams, Three Ways

Letniye fruktovyye dzhemy

At the end of summer, Mum would often get boxes of plums and peaches to preserve. She would either dry the fruit, make fruit wine (*nalivka*) or these delicious jams. The technique of boiling and then cooling jam three times is a common and a gentle way to keep the texture while the fruit cooks. I usually don't skin stone fruit when jam-making; I think the skin adds colour, flavour, a slight sourness and helps hold the fruit's shape when cooked down. Store these jams in the refrigerator.

MAKES ABOUT 2 x 500G (1LB 2OZ) JARS

1kg (2lb 4oz) yellow peaches, washed, dried, stoned and quartered
350g (12oz) sugar
2 handfuls of walnuts, chopped into bite-sized pieces

PEACH AND WALNUT JAM | *VARENYE IZ PERSIKOV I GRETSKIKH OREKHOV*
Walnuts add a subtle bitterness that complements the rich sweetness of the peaches. The amber-gold colour makes it almost too beautiful to open the jar. I also really like its texture – a reminder that I'm eating homemade jam.

First sterilize your jars (see page 62). Put the peaches and sugar in a large saucepan and stir through 2 tablespoons of water. Leave to stand for 1 hour, stirring occasionally.

Place the pan over a medium–high heat, bring to the boil, then turn off the heat. Let the mixture cool to room temperature, then bring back to the boil, turn off the heat and let cool again. Add the walnuts and return the jam to the boil for a third time, then immediately transfer the jam to the sterilized jars. Tightly seal with the lids and turn the jars upside down. Leave to cool fully overnight. Store in the refrigerator.

**MAKES ABOUT 2 x 500G
(1LB 2OZ) JARS**

1kg (2lb 4oz) plums, washed, dried,
  stoned and quartered
350g (12oz) sugar

PLUM JAM | *SLIVOVOYE VARENYE*

You can serve this jam over ice cream, use it as a filling
for plum biscuits, or simply as a spread on bread and
butter. You can also add walnuts to this jam, if you like.
Less is more with plums, I think. Choose beautifully ripe
plums, if you can.

First sterilize your jars (see page 62). Put the plums and sugar
in a large saucepan and stir through 2 tablespoons of water.
Leave to stand for 1 hour, occasionally stirring the mixture to
give the juices a head start – useful if the plums are not as ripe
as you'd like.

Place the pan over a medium–high heat, bring to the boil, then
turn off the heat. Let the mixture cool to room temperature,
then bring back to the boil, turn off the heat and let cool again.
Return the jam to the boil for a third time, then immediately
transfer the jam to the sterilized jars. Tightly seal with the lids
and turn the jars upside down. Leave to cool fully overnight.
Store in the refrigerator.

Pictured on the previous page with Peach and Walnut Jam.

Preservation

MAKES ABOUT 4 x 500G (1LB 2OZ) JARS

2kg (4lb 8oz) fresh whole strawberries, hulled, washed and then dried with paper towels
800g (1lb 12oz) sugar

WHOLE STRAWBERRY JAM | *KLUBNICHNOYE VARENYE*
Using fresh, sweet-smelling, in-season strawberries is ideal for this jam – overripe ones will just disintegrate and lose their shape quickly.

First sterilize your jars (see page 62). Transfer the strawberries to a large saucepan, add the sugar and toss to coat. Set aside for 1 hour, occasionally stirring the mixture gently.

Place the pan over a medium–high heat, bring to the boil, then turn off the heat. Let the mixture cool to room temperature, then bring back to the boil, turn off the heat and let cool again. Return the jam to the boil for a third time, then immediately transfer the jam to the sterilized jars. Tightly seal with the lids and turn the jars upside down. Leave to cool fully overnight. Store in the refrigerator.

Sour Cherry Preserve
Višniovaha varennia

Opening a jar of sweet and sour cherries during a cold winter in Belarus is an unforgettable food memory – a burst of summer joy in your mouth while it's miserable and dark outside. Often served with tea, preserves like this are laid out when guests come over unexpectedly. I nearly always keep a jar of this in my refrigerator, adding it to recipes here and there. It's quite a runny preserve – sour cherries release a lot of juice while cooking.

MAKES 4 x 250ML (9FL OZ) JARS

1kg (2lb 4oz) sour cherries, pitted
   (defrosted if frozen)
450g (1lb) sugar
100ml (3½fl oz) water

First sterilize your jars (see page 62). Place the cherries, sugar and water in a large saucepan. Stir together, cover with a lid and leave for about 1 hour.

Bring to the boil, then simmer for 5 minutes over the lowest heat, before turning it off completely. Let the mixture cool to room temperature. Repeat twice, and after the third boil, transfer the jam to the sterilized jars, tightly seal with the lids and turn upside down. Leave to cool fully overnight, then store in the refrigerator.

Tip: For a thicker consistency, after the third boil, reduce to a medium heat and cook for 15–20 minutes, stirring occasionally; however, do note that the jam thickens more when it cools down.

Eastern European Drinks, Three Ways

Uzvar | Mors | Kompot

The abundance of fruits grown in Belarus and Ukraine means people have found many ways to preserve the beautiful seasonal produce. Drinks such as these are a popular option. Here are a few favourites using redcurrants, cranberries and dried fruit, but do use what's seasonal or available to you and experiment with your own fruit combination. Traditionally, for kompots intended to keep, the fruit is kept in the jars as the flavour strengthens over time. Adjust the amount of sugar to your taste.

MAKES 1 LITRE (35FL OZ)

400g (14oz) dried mixed fruit such as
    pitted prunes or apricots, apples
    and raisins
1 cinnamon stick (optional)
1 litre (35fl oz) boiling water
2 Tbsp honey

MIXED DRIED FRUIT | *UZVAR IZ SUKHOFRUKTIV*
The traditional method for making uzvar is through infusion; letting it stand overnight rather than boiling the fruit. It is very popular in Ukraine, made with warming spices as a winter drink.

First sterilize a 1-litre (35fl oz) jar (see page 62). Place the fruit and cinnamon stick in a medium saucepan. Pour the measured boiling water and honey into the pan, cover with a lid and leave overnight.

The following day, strain the uzvar through a sieve into the jar, discarding the fruit. It's ready to drink straight away, warmed or cool, or seal tightly with the lid and store in the refrigerator for up to a week.

Preservation

MAKES 1 LITRE (35FL OZ)

1 litre (35fl oz) water
230g (8oz) cranberries (fresh or frozen)
3 Tbsp sugar or honey (optional)

CRANBERRY | *ŽURAVINAVY MORS*

Follow the method for the redcurrant kompot, below. Add a few whole cranberries at the end, if you like.

Pictured above.

MAKES 1 LITRE (35FL OZ)

1 litre (35fl oz) water
200g (7oz) redcurrants (sprigs removed)
3–4 Tbsp sugar or honey (optional)

REDCURRANT | *KRASNYY SMORODINOVYY KOMPOT*

Pour the measured water into a medium pan. Turn the heat on high and add the redcurrants and sugar (if you're using honey as the sweetener, add it at the end). Bring to the boil, then reduce the heat to a simmer. Cook, uncovered, for 5–10 minutes, then remove from the heat and leave to stand, covered, for at least 15 minutes to infuse the flavours. Drink warm or cool, and store in the refrigerator for up to 2 weeks. You can remove the cooked fruits or leave them as they are.

Variation: Sour cherries also make a delicious kompot. Just swap the redcurrants for 200g (7oz) of pitted sour cherries.

Together

Together

Recipes made to share

Much as I love cooking alone, I equally love occasions where I'm in a busy, messy kitchen or at a table with others prepping ingredients – picking herbs or filling cabbage leaves or blinchiki – while at the same time drinking coffee or wine and catching up. Each person with their own task, one maybe peeling vegetables, another rolling out dough, a third shaping and then cooking. I see these shared activities not as chores but as precious moments.

Whether frying *chebureky* (lamb turnovers) with my dad, or standing outdoors helping my brother cook *shashlyk* (lamb skewers), or sitting around a table with family and friends preparing wild blueberry *varenyky* (dumplings), it is always such a simple pleasure to cook together. You can easily make these recipes by yourself, but I think these dishes were *made* for cooking with others, and I hope you enjoy the process of making them as much as I do.

Ukrainian Dumplings, Three Ways

Varenyky

There are many variations of dumplings in Eastern Europe and one of the most common are Ukrainian varenyky, which translates best as 'boiled things'. The dough sometimes uses kefir or soured milk and can be made savoury or sweet. Fillings vary with the season and there are regional specialities, but ours usually consist of ingredients like potatoes, cabbage, sauerkraut, mushrooms, sour cherries or wild blueberries.

There's often a bag of homemade varenyky in our freezer because we tend to make more than we need. I recommend making a few different fillings so that you can try a bit of each. We love them with a coating of butter and lots of fried onion. The three savoury fillings here are my favourite; there's a recipe for sweet varenyky too on page 118.

MAKES 50-60

filling(s) of your choice
(see pages 98–99)

For the dough
700g (1lb 9oz) plain (all-purpose) flour,
plus extra for kneading
2 generous pinches of salt, plus extra
for cooking the dumplings
625ml (21fl oz) kefir
1 tsp bicarbonate of soda (baking soda)
1 tsp apple cider vinegar

First prepare your filling(s) and allow to cool.

To make the dough, put the flour in a large bowl and stir through the salt, then add the kefir. Mix the bicarbonate of soda and vinegar together until it's fizzing, then add to the bowl. Mix everything together with a fork, then use your hands to knead it a little in the bowl.

Flour your work surface and transfer the dough to it. Knead, adding more flour if it feels too sticky. Continue to knead until the dough is no longer grainy and feels soft. Place the dough on a plate, cover with cling film (plastic wrap) and leave on the worktop for at least 15 minutes.

Re-flour your work surface and lightly flour a tray or board too. Slice the dough into four pieces. Cover the pieces and roll out, one at a time, to about 3mm (⅛in) – not too thin. Use a cup to cut out circles, around 8cm (3¼in) in diameter. Place a heaped teaspoon of your cooled filling on one side. Close and seal the edges together to form half-moon shapes. Place on the floured tray while you make the rest.

Three-quarters fill an extra-large saucepan with water and bring to the boil. Season with salt. Once simmering, add the varenyky in batches, around 15 at a time. If you have an extra saucepan, you could cook two batches at once. Cook them until they rise to the surface, then remove with a slotted spoon.

Transfer the varenyky to a large bowl and follow the instructions on pages 98–99 for serving.

Together

Together

FOR THE POTATO FILLING AND FRIED ONION SAUCE

1kg (2lb 4oz) potatoes, peeled and
   quartered (depending on size)
70g (2½oz) butter, plus extra for coating
4 onions, finely sliced in half-moons
salt and pepper
soured cream, to serve

Put the potatoes into a saucepan of cold water and bring to the boil. Cook for 10–15 minutes or until fully cooked. Drain through a sieve, saving 250ml (9fl oz) of the water – discard the rest. Return the potatoes to the pan and add 25g (1oz) of the butter and the reserved potato water. Season very generously with salt and pepper. Mash until creamy and set aside to cool before filling the varenyky.

To make the sauce, place a frying pan over a medium–high heat and melt the remaining butter. Add the onions and cook, stirring often, adjusting the heat if it's too high. Add a generous pinch of salt and cook for 15–20 minutes.

Toss a few extra pieces of butter into the bowl of cooked varenyky and toss them to coat. Serve with the fried onion sauce and dollops of soured cream.

Together

FOR THE CABBAGE, SAUERKRAUT AND ONION FILLING

600g (1lb 5oz) cabbage, stem removed (about ¼ large cabbage), thinly sliced or shredded
50g (1¾oz) butter, plus extra for coating
1 onion, finely diced
380g (13½oz) sauerkraut
soured cream, to serve

Chop the sliced or shredded cabbage into smaller pieces. This will help keep it more compact when filling.

Place a large frying pan over a medium–high heat and add 25g (1oz) of the butter. Once melted, add the cabbage and onion. Cook, stirring often, for 10 minutes. Add the sauerkraut along with some of its brine – it is quite salty, so don't add extra seasoning at this point. Cook, stirring often, for about 20 minutes or more until the mixture is golden, the cabbage crispy and delicate. Add the rest of the butter as it cooks. Taste and adjust for seasoning if necessary. Set aside to cool before filling the varenyky.

Toss a few extra pieces of butter into the bowl of cooked varenyky and toss through to coat. Serve with dollops of soured cream.

FOR THE CHEESE FILLING

1kg (2lb 4oz) tvorog or cottage cheese
salt
butter, for coating
soured cream, to serve

In a bowl, mix the tvorog with 2 generous pinches of salt. Set aside ready for use.

Add a few pieces of butter into the bowl of cooked varenyky and toss through to coat. Serve with dollops of soured cream.

Tip: To freeze varenyky, place them on a tray and into the freezer for at least 1 hour until frozen. Transfer to a container or plastic bag and store in the freezer for a few months.

Stuffed Sweet and Sour Onions in Plum Sauce

Farshirovanyy luk s slivovym sousom

Just like my babushka Liana, I love to add plums or prunes to my recipes, and these onions are no exception. You could add more plum jam for extra sweetness (see the recipe on page 86), but I find this a nice balance of sweet and sour.

SERVES 6–8 WITH SIDES

5 medium–large onions, peeled
1 large bunch of parsley, finely chopped
1 large carrot, grated
500g (1lb 2oz) minced (ground) meat
  (beef, pork, lamb, or a mix)
210g (7½oz) jasmine rice
400ml (14fl oz) passata
1 Tbsp sweet paprika
1 Tbsp plum jam (jelly)
250g (9oz) pitted prunes
golden unrefined sunflower oil
  or other oil, for drizzling
salt and pepper

Bring a full kettle of water to the boil. For the onions, cut off the tips at both ends and from the root end, carve out the centre of the onion, so that the layers can come apart. Next, stand the onion on its end, place the tip of your knife in the centre of the rings and slice down the length of one side, so that each layer is now 'open'. Place into a large heatproof bowl and pour over the boiling water. Cover with a lid and leave for 30–40 minutes.

Once the onions have softened, remove from the water. Peel off each layer, trying to keep them intact. Set aside the smaller centre layers for the filling. Aim to have around 18 largish onion layers, or however many, once stuffed, will fit in your pan.

To make the filling, finely chop the reserved onion centres and place in a mixing bowl with the parsley, carrot, meat and rice. Season with salt and pepper and mix thoroughly.

Preheat the oven to 180°C fan/200°C/400°F/Gas mark 6. Add the passata, paprika, jam and 1 litre (35fl oz) of water to a separate bowl. Season and stir through. Spread some of this sauce on the bottom of a large ovenproof casserole dish, to cover it. Fill each onion layer with about 1 heaped tablespoon of the filling and place into the dish, arranging each stuffed onion side by side. Pour over the rest of the sauce. Tuck the prunes between each stuffed onion, pushing them in slightly. Drizzle with oil, then transfer to the oven and bake for 45 minutes or until the sauce has slightly reduced and the tops look darkened. Check the rice and meat filling from an onion in the centre is cooked. Serve and enjoy.

Cabbage Rolls
Holubtsi

Spend an afternoon with a friend making a large batch of these holubtsi.
For the filling, a mix of beef and pork mince works well, but I sometimes
make these with just beef – I use a really hearty beef mince mixture from
one of my butchers that includes liver, heart and other parts. I love to add
cayenne pepper, fresh herbs and lots of smetana (see page 15) or soured
cream, which helps balance the acidity of the tomato sauce. These cabbage
rolls can also be cooked on the stovetop in a large pot or Dutch oven.

SERVES 6–8

1 large cabbage, extra-thick, large outer
   leaves trimmed
1 small onion, finely diced
1kg (2lb 4oz) minced (ground) meat
   (50:50 beef and pork)
100g (3½oz) jasmine rice
1 large carrot, coarsely grated
500ml (17fl oz) passata
salt and pepper

To serve
1 Tbsp soured cream, plus extra
   (or crème fraîche)
golden unrefined sunflower oil
   or other oil
cayenne pepper or chilli flakes (or
   adjika if you have any, see page 17)
½ bunch of fresh dill, fronds chopped

Preheat the oven to 180°C fan/200°C/400°F/Gas mark 6
and line a large tray with paper towels. Bring a large saucepan
of water to the boil. Add a generous amount of salt. Carefully
cut in and around the stem of the cabbage to release the
leaves. Using your hands, remove each leaf carefully one by
one (don't worry too much if some tear). Continue to cut the
leaves at the stem as you work through the layers. Once I get
about two-thirds through the cabbage, I set the rest of it aside
as the central part has quite small leaves – I save it to cook at
a later time.

Rinse and blanch the leaves, in batches, in the simmering
salted water. To do this, use tongs to drop around three leaves
into the pan, then gently press to submerge. Blanch for around
3–4 minutes. Once blanched, transfer to the lined tray. Reserve
the water in the pan.

Once slightly cooled, take each leaf and cut a triangular wedge
(about 2cm/¾in) out of the thick stalk – removing this makes
it easier to roll the leaves.

Recipe continues overleaf.

Together

Together

To make the filling, put the onion, minced meat and rice in a bowl. Add 4 tablespoons of water and season with salt and pepper. Give it a really good mix.

For the sauce, put the carrot and passata in a large mixing jug. Add 2 large pinches of salt and 750ml (26fl oz) of water. Spoon about 4 tablespoons of this onto the base of a large ovenproof tray or casserole dish.

Place one cabbage leaf on a board. Put about 2 tablespoons of the filling in the centre close to the stem end. Fold that end over the filling, then bring the two sides to the centre and continue to roll it up to form a log shape. Continue with the rest. (If any leaves are really big, cut them in half before filling.)

Place enough rolls side by side in the tray to form a single layer. Cover with a generous amount of the sauce, then repeat with more layers of cabbage rolls and pour more of the sauce over. Once you've used all the rolls and sauce, pour in enough of the reserved blanching water to cover the cabbage rolls. Cover the tray with foil (or the lid if you're using a dish). Bake in the oven for 1½ hours, checking after 1 hour that there's enough water – add a bit more if needed. When nearly ready, check that the rice is cooked through by cutting into one cabbage roll. Cook for a little longer if you find it needs it.

Serve 2–3 cabbage rolls per person along with a few spoonfuls of the sauce. Top with a good dollop of soured cream, a drizzle of oil, a sprinkle of cayenne pepper or chilli, fresh dill, and cracked black pepper.

Pictured on previous page.

Crimean Lamb Turnovers
Chebureky

The word *burek* means 'pie' in several languages. Chebureky are a crescent-shaped snack popular all over Ukraine, first introduced by Crimean Tartars. Growing up, my dad would often stop by a *cheburechna* (a café that makes these turnovers) after school before heading home. Now I make these with Dad. The recipe is best done with two people: one fills and shapes and the other fries. We use lamb and ghee, but they can be made with other meats and cooked in different fats. Before you start cooking, check that you have a pan large enough to accommodate the size of these; if not, make smaller ones.

SERVES 4–6 (MAKES 12–14)

500g (1lb 2oz) plain (all-purpose) flour, sifted, plus extra for kneading
1 egg
250ml (9fl oz) just-boiled water
2 Tbsp sunflower oil
ghee or sunflower oil, for cooking
salt and pepper
mustard, to serve

For the filling
2 large onions
375ml (13fl oz) water (or stock)
700g (1lb 9oz) minced (ground) lamb

Put the flour and 1 teaspoon of salt in a large mixing bowl. Whisk the egg in a cup and then add it to the flour with the just-boiled water and the oil. Use a fork to stir the mixture roughly together, then transfer to a lightly floured work surface and knead for 5 minutes. Shape into a ball, place in a bowl and cover. Set aside to rest for 15 minutes.

Meanwhile make the filling. Blend the onions and the water in a small blender. Put the lamb mince in a separate bowl with two generous pinches of salt and a pinch of pepper. Pour in the onion mixture. Use a fork to mix it initially, then use your hands to thoroughly mix it together, adding more water if needed – the consistency should be quite wet.

Cut the rested dough into 12 pieces each roughly 65g (2¼oz). Cover with cling film (plastic wrap).

Recipe continues overleaf.

Lightly flour the work surface. Take one piece of dough and roll into a thin circle roughly 18cm (7in) in diameter. Place a medium-sized plate on top and use a knife to cut around the plate. Repeat with a few more dough pieces so that you have a few ready to cook, keeping the rest covered so that they don't begin to dry out. Reserve the offcuts and keep those covered, too – they can be combined and rolled out at the end to make extras.

Line a baking tray with baking paper – don't be tempted to dust with flour as that will burn when cooking.

Place one of your rolled-out dough circles on the tray with the stickier side up and add 1 tablespoon of the filling just to one side of the centre. You don't need to spread it. Fold over the other half of the dough to create a crescent shape. Press the edges together with your fingers then press with a fork so that they stick firmly together. Once you have at least two prepared, you can begin to cook them.

Heat a large frying pan over a medium–high heat. Add a tablespoon of ghee or enough oil to cover the base of the pan. Once hot, place the chebureky into the pan, two at a time, fitting them in together. Cook for about 1½ minutes on each side: you want the pastry crispy with visible air bubbles and, when you bite into it, a juicy filling. Use a spatula to help you flip the chebureky carefully, adjusting the heat and amount of ghee or oil as you need.

Once cooked, transfer the chebureky onto a plate or tray lined with paper towel while you make and cook the rest. Allow them to cool just slightly – the filling will be very hot – and serve with as much mustard as you like.

Tip: If you have any leftover filling, you can use it to make the Stuffed Chicken Rissoles (see page 169).

Lamb Skewers

Shashlyk

Shashlyk is popular all over Eastern Europe and is perfect for cooking outdoors. The smell of lamb skewers cooking over hot coals draws everyone in. You will need a charcoal grill for these, a bag of coals and some large skewers. I've tried to create a recipe that clearly explains how to make shashlyk step by step, but keep in mind that grills vary, as does the amount of heat coming off the coals. Any charcoal grill will be fine, but shashlyk are traditionally cooked on a mangal – these are fairly easy to source online. Start this recipe the evening before you plan to cook the skewers.

MAKES 10-12 LARGE SKEWERS

6 large onions, sliced into rings
   about 5mm (¼in) thick
375ml (13fl oz) white vinegar
   (3% strength)
1 leg of lamb (about 1.5kg/3lb 5oz)
salt and pepper

To serve
flatbreads
platter of spring onions (scallions),
   fresh coriander (cilantro), cucumbers,
   tomatoes or other salad ingredients
Adjika (page 78), hot sauce or
   Aubergine Ikra (page 160)

The night before, you need to brine the meat and onions. As you slice the onions, try to keep the rings complete so that the layers don't separate. Remove the outermost layer of some of the largest onion rings, and place these in a large bowl with 2 litres (70fl oz) of water, the vinegar, 4 generous pinches of salt and 2 pinches of pepper.

Slice the meat off the bone, then cut into roughly 5cm (2in) cubes. Add to the bowl and mix. Carefully place the smaller, intact onion rings on top and around the meat – some may break, but try to keep them whole. Cover the bowl and leave in the refrigerator overnight, ideally for 10–15 hours. The next day, remove the bowl and allow to come up to room temperature before you start your grill.

Prepare your grill as for any barbecue. Fill it with coals, light them and allow it to get to a medium–high temperature, with no flames, and for the coals to be greyish-white. Timing is key: once the coals are ready, they need to last for at least 20–30 minutes with consistent heat.

Meanwhile, get 10–12 large metal skewers, then start to skewer the meat, placing a few compact onion rings in between each piece of meat. The larger rings can also be skewered; simply fold them into a figure-eight shape and then fold again so that you have a double ring. Aim for about five pieces of meat per skewer, depending on how large your grill is – it's important there's enough space for you to grip the skewers with your hands to rotate them.

Place the skewers onto the grill and cook for about 10 minutes on each side, turning them often. Use the leftover onion brine to pour over the coals whenever you see any flames come up – you want to avoid any strong flames.

Cook to your liking, try one before you take them all off the grill and adjust the seasoning and cook for longer as needed.

Serve the meat and charred onions alongside flatbreads, salads and sauce.

Together

Blinchiki with Slow-cooked Meat

Blinchiki s myasom

Filled, rolled blinchiki with slow-cooked meat, pan-fried in butter and hot off the pan are a childhood favourite of many Eastern European families. You can also make these pancakes ahead of time and store them in a container in the refrigerator, ready to quickly pan-fry in butter and serve with soured cream.

SERVES 6–8 (MAKES ABOUT 16–18)

1 x quantity Eastern European Pancakes batter (page 21)
soured cream, to serve

For the filling
1kg (2lb 4oz) chuck steak (or 2 x 500g/ 1lb 2oz pieces)
2 onions, 1 whole and 1 diced
1 bay leaf
20g (¾oz) butter, plus extra for frying the blinchiki
1 carrot, grated
salt and pepper

First make the filling. Fill a large saucepan three-quarters full with water, then add the meat along with the whole onion, bay leaf and a pinch of salt, ensuring the water covers the meat. Cover the pan, place over a medium heat and gently simmer for about 2 hours or until the meat is soft and tender. Remove the meat from the pan (reserving the broth), cool and then finely chop the meat or use a food processor to shred.

Melt the butter in a large pan over a medium–high heat and cook the diced onion and grated carrot for 7–10 minutes until soft and golden. Add the shredded meat and a ladleful or two of the reserved broth. Season with salt and pepper and cook for 5 minutes. Turn off the heat and set aside.

Meanwhile make enough batter for 16–18 blinchiki following the method on page 21.

Place one of the blinchiki on a board and add 2 tablespoons of the meat filling to the centre. Fold the bottom edge over the filling, then the sides, and fold into a rectangular parcel. Repeat with the rest.

To cook, melt some butter in a frying pan and, when hot and sizzling, pan-fry the blinchiki a few at a time until crispy and golden on both sides. Serve immediately, 2–3 per person, with a dollop of soured cream.

Baked Hand Pies
with Meat
Zapechennyye pirozhki s myasom

Mum would often serve these baked hand pies alongside the rich, meaty broth that's created when making the filling. These are also nice alongside any other soup. A labour of love, these pies are often made in large batches – they freeze well so any leftovers can be stored and easily reheated. Usually the filling is prepared ahead of time. Here it's made with chuck steak but you can use any cut of meat that is suitable for slow cooking.

SERVES 6–8 (MAKES ABOUT 40)

500ml (17fl oz) lukewarm milk
3 Tbsp sugar
14g (½oz) fast-action dried yeast
1kg (2lb 4oz) plain (all-purpose) flour,
    plus extra as needed
2 tsp salt
160g (5¾oz) butter, melted
4 eggs at room temperature, beaten
egg wash (1 egg beaten with a generous
    splash of milk)

For the filling
1kg (2lb 4oz) chuck steak
2 onions, 1 whole, 1 diced
1 bay leaf
20g (¾oz) butter
2 carrots, grated
salt and pepper

First, make the filling. Put the chuck steak in a large stockpot with the whole onion, the bay leaf, 3 litres (105fl oz) of water and a pinch of salt. Place over a medium heat, cover and reduce to a simmer for about 2 hours, occasionally skimming the surface to remove any impurities.

Once the meat is tender and soft, remove from the pot (reserving the broth) and cool. Finely chop or shred the meat and set aside in a bowl.

Melt the butter in a large frying pan over a medium–high heat, add the diced onion and cook stirring occasionally until golden and translucent, about 5 minutes. Add the carrots and stir through until softened and cooked through. Add the meat and season with salt and pepper. Cook, stirring, for 5 minutes, then add 2 ladlefuls of the broth and turn off the heat. Taste and adjust the seasoning. Cover with a lid.

Prepare the dough when you are ready to cook the pirozhki. In a jug, stir together the lukewarm milk, sugar, yeast and 4 tablespoons of the flour. Set aside for the yeast to become frothy.

Sift the rest of the flour into the bowl of a stand mixer fitted with a dough hook. Stir through the salt. Pour in the yeast mixture, the melted butter and the beaten eggs. Mix for around 5–10 minutes or until the dough has come together and is smooth. Add up to 150g (5½oz) extra flour if it looks too moist.

Together

You can also make the dough by hand – just mix the ingredients in a bowl and knead until smooth. Transfer the dough to a lightly floured or oiled bowl and cover. Leave to rise until it has doubled in size.

Preheat the oven to 180°C fan/200°C/400°F/Gas mark 6. Line a couple of baking trays with baking paper. Remove the dough from the bowl and cut off a quarter. Keep the remainder covered so that it doesn't dry out. Divide the quarter into pieces each weighing roughly 45–50g (1¾oz). Flour your work surface and roll the pieces into circles about 10cm (4in) in diameter. Add around 1 heaped tablespoon of the filling into the centre of each disc, then gather the edges and pinch to seal. Flip the pies over and shape into an oval. Place the hand pies on the lined trays, spaced apart, and continue to shape, roll and fill the rest of the dough. Cover with cling film (plastic wrap) as you make them.

Once all the pies are filled and shaped, brush the tops with egg wash and cook in batches for 15–20 minutes or until the tops are golden, then carefully stack them in a large bowl and cover with a dish towel; they will continue to soften in the steam as they cool down. Serve fresh from the oven with some of the remaining meat stock or soup on the side, if you like.

Fried Hand Pies,
Three Ways
Smazheni Pyrizhky

When babushka Liana emigrated from Ukraine to join us in Sydney, she brought many recipes with her. She gave me a detailed description of how her mum, Zinaida, would make these pyrizhky. Babushka would use either foraged or homegrown greens like dill, spring onion and parsley.

When making these, you can prepare all three fillings if you wish; just divide the ingredients by three. Serve hot off the pan as they are, or you could even serve these alongside soups; for example, the potato and mushroom pyrizhky are delicious served with Vegetable and Bean Borsch (page 127).

**SERVES 4–6 AS A SNACK
(MAKES 14–16)**

For the dough
50ml (1¾fl oz) sunflower oil,
  plus extra for frying
14g (½oz) fast-action dried yeast
50g (1¾oz) caster (granulated) sugar
500ml (17fl oz) lukewarm water
550g (1lb 4oz) plain (all-purpose) flour,
  sifted, plus extra for kneading
salt

filling(s) of your choice (see overleaf)

In a large mixing bowl whisk together the oil, yeast, sugar and 3 generous pinches of salt. Pour in the lukewarm water and mix through. Add the flour and mix to a sticky, rough-textured dough. (Alternatively, you can do this in a stand mixer fitted with a dough hook.)

Generously flour a work surface. Transfer the dough mixture onto the surface and sprinkle plenty of flour over the top. Flour your hands and then knead the dough for about 5 minutes. You may need to add a bit more flour: the dough should be soft, but not sticky.

Form the dough into a smooth round shape and place it into a lightly floured or oiled bowl. Cover with a plate or cling film (plastic wrap) and place in the refrigerator for 30 minutes.

Meanwhile prepare your filling(s) – see overleaf.

Once you have prepared your filling(s), remove the dough from the refrigerator. Use a knife to cut the dough into pieces weighing around 65g (2¼oz). Lightly flour the work surface again and flour a rolling pin and your hands. Roll the pieces out into long oval shapes, about 3mm (⅛in) thick.

Place about 2 heaped tablespoons of your filling into the centre of one of your rolled dough pieces. Bring the opposite edges of the dough together, pinching them to press the edges together. Shape to form an oval bun. Flip it and place on a lightly floured surface. Repeat until you have made at least three and then begin to cook them while you continue to fill and shape the rest.

Heat a large frying pan with a generous amount of oil over a medium–high heat. Cook the pyrizhky for a few minutes on each side until golden, adjusting the heat slightly as needed. Remove from the pan to a plate lined with paper towels while you fill and cook the rest. These are best served hot from the pan.

Recipe fillings overleaf.

FOR THE MIXED GREENS AND EGG FILLING

4 large eggs
large bunch of spinach, washed
    and trimmed
large bunch of spring onions (scallions),
    roughly chopped
large bunch of dill, soft fronds only,
    roughly chopped
large bunch of parsley, leaves only,
    roughly chopped
salt

Place the eggs in a small saucepan of cold water over a medium heat. Cover with a lid and bring to a gentle boil. Reduce the heat to a simmer and cook the eggs for about 9 minutes. Remove from the heat, strain the hot water and refill the pan with cold water. Leave the eggs to cool.

Meanwhile, place all of the chopped greens in a large mixing bowl. Peel then roughly chop the eggs and add to the greens. Season with lots of salt and mix thoroughly.

FOR THE CABBAGE, CARROT AND ONION FILLING

70g (2½oz) butter, ghee or oil
½ medium cabbage, finely sliced
    or shredded
1 onion, finely sliced
1 large carrot, grated
200g (7oz) sauerkraut (or more,
    if you prefer)
salt

Place a large, lidded frying pan over a medium–high heat and melt about 3 tablespoons of the butter. Add the cabbage and a splash of water. Cook, stirring, for 5 minutes or until the cabbage reduces slightly. Add the onion, carrot and a pinch of salt. Cover the pan and cook gently for 10 minutes over a medium heat.

After 10 minutes, remove the lid, stir in the sauerkraut and the rest of the butter. Increase the heat and cook for 10–15 minutes or until the mixture is reduced by half, and the cabbage and onion are nicely golden. You can cook this for longer but I do like the filling to have a bit of texture to it. Taste and add more salt if needed.

FOR THE POTATO AND MUSHROOM FILLING

1.5kg (3lb 5oz) potatoes, peeled
70g (2½oz) butter, ghee or oil
1 onion, diced
800g (1lb 12oz) mushrooms,
    finely chopped
salt

Place the potatoes in a large saucepan of water, seasoned with salt, and bring to a boil.

Meanwhile, place a medium frying pan over a medium–high heat and melt 2 tablespoons of the butter. Add the onion and mushrooms and cook, stirring often, for 10 minutes or until the mushrooms have reduced and are starting to catch on the base of the pan. Season with a pinch of salt.

Once the potatoes are cooked, strain off three-quarters of the water, but leave the rest in the pan. Mash the potatoes directly in the water, adding the rest of the butter. Stir through the cooked mushroom mix, taste and season accordingly.

Together

Steamed Varenyky with Wild Blueberries

Varenyky na paru z lisovoyu chornytseyu

When summer comes to Ukraine and Belarus and wild blueberries cover the forest floor, everyone wants blueberry varenyky. In Sydney, it wasn't always possible to find wild blueberries; though, these days, they're imported from Poland and sold frozen. In this recipe, we use frozen berries because, if they defrost, their juices can get quite messy. Berries are delicate, so steaming them is our preferred method; steam also makes the dough slightly fluffier.

We often prepare these outdoors together in the summer. If you don't have a steamer basket, you can improvise by tying a piece of muslin cloth (cheesecloth) over the pot, just like we would do at babushka Lida's dacha. Add more sugar if you like – we just add it by eye, it doesn't have to be exact.

SERVES 4 (MAKES ABOUT 40)

800g (1lb 12oz) plain (all-purpose) flour, plus extra for dusting
1 tsp salt
500ml (17fl oz) kefir at room temperature
1 tsp bicarbonate of soda (baking soda)
100ml (3½fl oz) soured cream, plus extra to serve

For the filling
800g (1lb 12oz) frozen wild blueberries
210g (7½oz) caster (superfine) sugar
80g (2¾oz) butter, for coating

First make the dough. Put the flour and salt in one large bowl. In a second large bowl, mix the kefir and bicarbonate of soda together, add the soured cream and combine thoroughly. Pour this mixture into the bowl of flour. Mix roughly, then use your hands to bring the mixture together and start to knead it in the bowl.

Lightly flour your work surface and roll out the dough to about 3mm (⅛in) thick – don't roll it too thinly as you want the dough to be able to keep the blueberries inside. Use an upturned glass (about 8cm/3¼in diameter) to cut out circles from the rolled-out dough. As you press out the shapes, start to fill them. Take half the batch of wild blueberries from the freezer (keeping the rest inside so they don't defrost quickly).

Place a heaped teaspoon of the wild blueberries into one half of each circle, sprinkle with a third of a teaspoon of sugar, then fold into a half-moon shape, pressing down lightly to seal the edges. Crimp the edges with your fingers. Set aside on a lightly floured board or tray. Continue to fill the varenyky, taking more frozen blueberries as you need from the freezer.

Set up a steamer basket or muslin cloth (cheesecloth) over a saucepan filled with water and bring to the boil. When ready, place a few varenyky in the steamer – about 7–8 or however many fit without being squashed: they do puff up a bit. Cover with a lid and steam for 3–4 minutes or until the varenyky have fluffed up and you can see some of the blueberry colour coming through the dough. The exact cooking time varies so take out one varenyky and slice in half to check the pastry is cooked through – you shouldn't see any raw dough.

Meanwhile, warm the butter and add a tablespoon to a large bowl where you'll place the steamed varenyky. Use this to coat the varenyky so that they don't stick together. Pour over another tablespoon of butter each time a new batch is ready. Serve the varenyky immediately, coated in the butter and with extra soured cream on top.

Together

Together

Savoury & Comforting

Savoury & Comforting

Recipes to take your time with

Cooking that takes time can sometimes set you up for the week ahead. I love the feeling of slowing down, especially on weekends when I can find a couple of hours to myself. Take the chicken stock, for example. Having that base stored in your refrigerator or freezer is a blessing, as you can then use it to make quick and delicious meals when time is of the essence.

My babushka Liana used to make borsch on Sundays. It was her way of ending one week and preparing for the next – essential for feeding the whole family when we all lived together in Ukraine. She would use what she had and so, depending on the season, her borsch would vary slightly.

These are the dishes to cook when you might want to take a slower pace in the kitchen, whether it's wintry and raining outside, or because you feel like a bit of a kitchen reset, or simply because you just feel like cooking. All require a bit of time and patience, but the flavour makes them so worth your while.

Borsch, Two Ways

M'yasnyy borshch / Pisnyi borshch

Most people are familiar with borsch. It is one of the most iconic dishes of Ukrainian and Eastern European cuisines. Reflecting moments in history, within regions and between generations, borsch is an ever-evolving and culturally significant dish. There are many variations of borsch, but from each it's possible to glimpse a snippet of the life of the person who shared it – of their environmental and cultural landscape. For me, and others who have left Eastern Europe, borsch is the dish that takes me home.

Borsch isn't hard to make, but it takes several stages to develop the flavour. Roasting beetroot develops its sweetness, and for the same reason I make a *zazharka* (also known as *zasmazhka*), which involves cooking onions and carrots in fat first. We finish borsch with fresh herbs and garlic, a dollop of soured cream and some cayenne pepper.

Savoury & Comforting

Meat Borsch
M'yasnyy borshch

For this we prepare a good rich meat broth as the base. Osso bucco contains fat, meat and marrow, so it's a great choice for making stock, as is oxtail, a traditional cut for borsch. Ideally, use a combination of cuts – perhaps also some bone marrow (halved lengthways) and rump steak. I often prep the stock and roast the beetroot the night before. Adding the beetroot at two different stages keeps its rich colour – the lemon juice helps too.

SERVES 8–10

1kg (2lb 4oz) osso bucco and oxtail
    (about 500g/1lb 2oz each, or include
    bone marrow or rump steak too)
2 onions, 1 whole, 1 diced
3 medium to large beetroots, unpeeled
30g (1oz) butter, ghee, oil or diced salo
1 carrot, grated
2 large potatoes, peeled and chopped
    into 2cm (¾in) chunks
½ red (bell) pepper, peeled and
    finely diced
2–3 Tbsp vinegar or lemon juice
250g (9oz) passata
1 heaped tablespoon adjika or red (bell)
    pepper paste (optional; see page 17)
wedge of cabbage (white or red),
    very thinly shredded or sliced
salt and pepper

To serve
2 garlic cloves, peeled
small handful of both dill and parsley,
    roughly chopped
2 tsp sunflower oil
bread and/or slices of salo (page 82)
soured cream
cayenne pepper (optional)

First make the meat stock. Put the meat into a large stockpot with the whole onion, 2 generous pinches of salt and 4 litres (140fl oz) of water. Bring to a simmer over a medium heat, skim off any impurities, then reduce the heat, cover with a lid and cook for 3 hours at the lowest possible simmer – this ensures the broth stays clear.

Meanwhile preheat the oven to 180°C fan/200°C/400°F/ Gas mark 6. Put the beetroots in a tray and roast for about 50 minutes. Pierce one with a skewer to check they are cooked right through. Remove from the oven, allow to cool then peel, grate and set aside.

After simmering for 3 hours, remove the meat from the stockpot, let it cool slightly on a board, then separate the meat from any bone or tough ligaments. Shred or chop the meat and softened ligaments into small pieces and set aside. If there is any bone marrow, scoop it out, chop into a paste and set aside. If you wish, strain the broth through a sieve into a clean large pot.

Now you can make the borsch. Heat a frying pan over a medium heat, add the butter, oil or cooking fat (if using salo, pan-fry for a few minutes to release the fat) and cook the diced onion and carrot for 7–10 minutes, stirring occasionally, until they have softened and taken on some colour.

Recipe continues overleaf.

Meanwhile, bring the pot of broth back to a gentle simmer over a low heat. Add the potatoes, red pepper and the onion and carrot mixture to the pot. Increase the heat to high, add the meat and any marrow paste and season with salt and pepper. Once boiling, add half the grated beetroot, the vinegar, the passata and adjika (if using). Cover with a lid and cook at a low–medium simmer. After about 10 minutes, check the potatoes are cooked. Add the cabbage and cook for 3 minutes, then add the remaining beetroot. Bring to the boil, cook for 2 minutes, then turn off the heat. Taste and adjust the seasoning. Cover with a lid and let stand for at least 30 minutes or overnight.

When you're ready to serve, roughly chop one of the garlic cloves. Add to a small bowl and mix with the dill, parsley, oil and a pinch of salt. Toast or grill your bread. Slice one end off the second garlic clove and rub over the bread.

Serve the borsch hot with the garlicky herb mixture, soured cream and cayenne pepper (if using) on top and the garlic-rubbed bread on the side. If you're not eating the borsch initially, its flavours fully develop over the following days and it does thicken with time – just add a splash of water when reheating it.

Savoury & Comforting

Vegetable and Bean Borsch

Pisnyi borshch

As a quicker option, the rich base flavour of vegetarian borsch is achieved by making a zazharka, which involves cooking onions and carrots in fat first. Trust me on the amount of garlic: roasting whole cloves softens and sweetens them. If you have time, presoak and precook dried beans instead of using canned. I love to serve this with fried pyrizhky (page 114).

SERVES 8-10

8 large garlic cloves: 6 unpeeled,
  2 crushed
1 whole red (bell) pepper
3 medium to large beetroots, unpeeled
sunflower oil, for drizzling
2 onions, finely diced
1 large carrot, grated
1 Tbsp adjika or red (bell) pepper paste
  (optional; see page 17)
400g (14oz) passata
1 green apple, cored and grated
2 x 400g (14oz) cans red kidney beans,
  drained and rinsed
1 bay leaf
1 tsp sweet paprika
½ tsp cayenne pepper (optional),
  plus extra to serve
600g (1lb 5oz) potatoes, peeled, cut
  into wedges and placed in a bowl
  of cold water
¼ cabbage (red or white),
  finely shredded
1 bunch of both parsley and dill,
  roughly chopped
salt and pepper

To serve
soured cream
fresh bread

Preheat the oven to 180°C fan/200°C/400°F/Gas mark 6. Put the 6 garlic cloves, the red pepper and the beetroots (keeping the skin on) on a large baking tray and drizzle a generous amount of oil over the garlic and pepper. Roast in the oven for 30 minutes or until the garlic and pepper have softened. Remove them from the tray, but continue to roast the beetroots for another 20 minutes. Discard the skins from the garlic and the pepper, along with its seeds and stem. Mash the garlic and finely dice the pepper on a board and combine to a paste-like consistency. Once the beetroots are cooked, cool slightly, peel and coarsely grate them.

Add a generous drizzle of oil to a large stockpot. Place over a medium–high heat and cook the onions and carrot for 7–10 minutes, stirring occasionally, or until they have softened and taken on some colour. Add the beetroot, the garlic-pepper paste, adjika (if using), passata, apple, beans, bay leaf, paprika and cayenne pepper (if using). Cover with 4 litres (140fl oz) of water and plenty of salt, to taste. Cover with a lid and cook over a low–medium heat for 15 minutes at a slight simmer. After the 15 minutes is up, drain the potatoes and add to the pot with the cabbage, and cook for a further 15 minutes.

Turn off the heat off and stir through the chopped herbs and crushed garlic. Taste and adjust the seasoning. Serve with soured cream, fresh bread and extra cayenne pepper if you wish.

Chicken Soup with Spelt Dumplings

Galushky sup

Galushky, or halushki, are Ukrainian dumplings, which I make with spelt flour. They can be served in different ways, one of which is to drop them into hot soup. They cook in minutes – ideal for when you want a quick and comforting meal and when you have shredded chicken and stock in the refrigerator. Choose any sort of small pasta or something thin like vermicelli.

SERVES 4

1.5 litres (52fl oz) chicken stock (see
   page 135 or use store-bought)
2 large potatoes, peeled and sliced into
   batons about 3cm (1¼in) long
1 carrot, grated
70g (2½oz) small pasta – I use stelline
   or vermicelli, but any small pasta
   will be fine
300g (10½oz) shredded chicken
   (more if you like)
large handful of dill fronds, chopped
salt and pepper

For the dumplings
1 egg
pinch of salt
1 Tbsp water
3 Tbsp spelt flour

Bring the chicken stock to a simmer in a medium saucepan. Add the potato batons and cook for 5 minutes, then add the grated carrot. After 2 minutes, stir through the pasta and shredded chicken, taste and season. Set a timer for 30 seconds less than the instructions given on the pasta packet – this will be your cue to add the dumplings.

Meanwhile, make the dumplings. In a medium bowl, mix the egg, salt and water, then add the flour and mix until smooth. The mixture will be quite liquid. With the soup still simmering, start to add teaspoonfuls of the galushky dough, one after the other, giving them a stir through. Once they float to the top, stir in the dill and turn off the heat.

Serve in bowls with freshly cracked black pepper.

Savoury & Comforting

Mixed Mushrooms and Buckwheat Soup

Gribnoy sup

If you're looking for something comforting to make one cold and rainy day, this earthy mushroom soup is what I'd recommend. Use any mushrooms you like, including frozen ones – if using frozen, no need to defrost, simply slice and add them straight from the freezer. I recommend using toasted buckwheat that can be found in Eastern European delis.

SERVES 4

100g (3½oz) toasted buckwheat (kasha)
1.5 litres (52fl oz) chicken stock (see page 135 or use store-bought)
2 large potatoes, peeled and sliced into batons about 3cm (1¼in) long
200–250g (7–9oz) fresh or frozen mushrooms, quartered or sliced into bite-sized pieces
1 carrot, grated
large handful of dill fronds, chopped
salt and pepper
soured cream, to serve

Rinse and drain the toasted buckwheat, then add to a medium saucepan and half-fill with room-temperature water. Bring to the boil, then drain through a sieve. Return the buckwheat to the pan, then refill with 250ml (9fl oz) of room-temperature water and season with salt. Bring to the boil again, then reduce the heat to keep it on a low simmer. Cover with a lid and cook for 10–15 minutes or until most of the water has been absorbed.

Meanwhile, pour the chicken stock into a separate saucepan and bring to a simmer. Add the potatoes and mushrooms, cook for 5 minutes, then add the grated carrot. Cook for a further 5 minutes. Once the potatoes are cooked through, stir in the buckwheat and cook for a final minute.

Add the dill, taste and season. Adjust with a splash of hot water if the soup is too dense for your liking.

Serve in bowls with freshly cracked black pepper and a dollop of soured cream if you wish.

Savoury & Comforting

Mushroom Stew with Buckwheat Blini

Hrybnaje mačanka i bliny z hrečki

I first had this mushroom stew when visiting a family friend in south Belarus. Like many, Luda – an incredible cook and artist – forages for mushrooms. One way she cooks with them is by making mačanka. Typically, mačanka is made with pork and served with blini; instead, she made it with a mixture of fresh and dried mushrooms that she had been preserving on her front porch. The earthy buckwheat blini pair beautifully with the rich stew.

SERVES 6 (MAKES 14 BLINI)

For the buckwheat blini
300g (10½oz) plain (all-purpose) flour
140g (5oz) buckwheat flour
3 pinches of salt
1 tsp sugar
1 egg
750ml (26fl oz) full-fat (whole) milk
1 tsp bicarbonate of soda (baking soda)
2 tsp apple cider vinegar
    (unfiltered preferably)
butter or ghee, for cooking

For the mačanka
10g (¼oz) dry porcini mushrooms
250ml (9fl oz) boiling water
100g (3½oz) butter
1 garlic clove, crushed
1 small onion or leek, finely chopped
700g (1lb 9oz) white button mushrooms
    or chestnut (Swiss) mushrooms,
    cleaned and quartered
handful of flat-leaf parsley,
    roughly chopped
leaves from 4 thyme sprigs
600ml (21fl oz) single (light) cream
1–2 Tbsp plain (all-purpose) flour
salt and pepper

For the blini, sift the flours into a large bowl. Whisk through the salt and sugar. In a separate bowl, whisk together the egg, milk and 250ml (9fl oz) water. In a cup, mix the bicarbonate of soda and vinegar until fizzing, then add this to the wet ingredients. Pour half the wet ingredients into the dry ingredients. Whisk well until a thick batter forms, gradually adding more of the wet ingredients and whisking so that the batter is smooth. Keep working the mixture to add air into the batter while hydrating the flour. Use a ladle to check the consistency. If it's too thick or too heavy, add more milk.

Place a medium cast-iron pan over a high heat. Add a knob of butter or ghee and let it melt (repeat this each time you add batter). Tilt the pan to spread the butter over the base. Add a ladleful of batter, tilting the pan from side to side so that the batter is evenly distributed. Reduce the heat to medium–high and place the pan back over the heat. Soon you should see air bubbles appearing. Cook for about 2 minutes, then use a spatula to flip the blini. Cook for only 1–2 minutes on the second side, adding more butter and adjusting the heat as needed. Repeat with the rest of the batter. Transfer them, one by one, to a plate and top with extra butter as you layer them up. Keep warm.

Recipe continues overleaf.

Savoury & Comforting

To make the mačhanka, soak the dried porcini in the boiling water. Meanwhile, place a large frying pan over a medium–high heat, add 50g (1¾oz) of the butter, the garlic and onion and cook, stirring occasionally, for about 5 minutes until the onion has softened. Reduce the heat slightly if the garlic starts to catch. Add the fresh mushrooms, the remaining butter and a pinch of salt. Cook, stirring occasionally, for 10 minutes until the mushrooms are slightly golden – you don't want them to completely cook down and all the liquid to evaporate as this is needed for the consistency and flavour of the sauce.

Once the mushrooms have some colour, add the soaked porcini along with the soaking liquid, the parsley and thyme. Pour in the cream, season generously and cook, covered with a lid, at a low simmer for 10 minutes. Remove the lid, increase the heat, add the flour and mix continuously until the sauce thickens. Taste and adjust the seasoning.

Serve the stew with the blini folded on top or alongside, ready to dip.

Savoury & Comforting

Mum's Chicken Stock

Kurinyy bul'on ot mamy

My mum often has a pot of chicken stock simmering away, filling the house with wonderful aromas. I have asked her again and again how she makes it so good. Her response is always: 'You have to really love chicken stock to make a good chicken stock.' Use an extra-large pot – around 5 litres capacity – and simmer it slowly over the lowest heat.

MAKES 4–5 LITRES (140–170FL OZ)

1 raw whole chicken
1 onion or the white part of a leek
1 carrot
1 small bay leaf
6–8 black peppercorns
a few sprigs of parsley, stems and leaves
1 parsnip root and 1 parsley root
   (optional)
½ celery stick (optional)
salt

Place the chicken into your biggest stockpot and fill with around 4 litres (140fl oz) water to cover. Bring to the boil and cook for 1 minute – you will start to see the froth on the surface of the water. Remove the chicken from the pot and give it a good wash under cold water. Discard the water from the pot and wash the pot as well. Return the chicken to the clean pot and refill with another 4–5 litres (140–170fl oz) water. Bring back to the boil and add 2 tablespoons of salt. Skim off any impurities that form on the surface of the water.

Add the remaining ingredients, reduce the heat to the lowest possible setting, cover with a lid and simmer gently for 1 hour, checking often that the stock is not simmering strongly.

Transfer the whole chicken onto a chopping board. Remove the chicken breast, place in a closed container to cool and keep in the refrigerator to use as you wish. Return the rest of the chicken to the pot. Add 1 tablespoon of salt, re-cover with the lid and continue to cook over a very low heat for another 2 hours.

After a total of 3 hours' cooking, turn the heat off. Cover with the lid and let the stock cool down in the pot for a few hours.

Remove and shred any of the cooked chicken meat and store in a container in the refrigerator (use in the soup on page 128). Remove the carcass, vegetables and herbs from the stock and strain through a sieve to remove any residual bits. Pour into jars, seal with a lid, cool, then store in the refrigerator, where it will keep for around a week, or freeze for up to 6 months.

Chicken and Potato Dill Stew

Kurinoye ragu s kartofelem i ukropom

This stew is similar to chicken soup but slightly more substantial. It has few ingredients and dill is the hero. The stew absorbs the liquid and develops flavour over time so you might need to add a bit more water if reheating over the following days. Use starchy potatoes that break down to create an almost creamy sauce. We typically enjoy this with friends in autumn or winter, served with plenty of fresh bread and vodka shots.

SERVES 6–8

60g (2¼oz) butter, plus an extra knob
1.2kg (2lb 12oz) chicken cuts such as thighs, drumsticks and wings, or a 1–1.3kg (2lb 4oz–3lb) whole chicken divided into portions
1 onion or leek, finely diced
2 carrots, thinly sliced into half-moons or quarters
1kg (2lb 4oz) potatoes, peeled and chopped into smallish pieces
1 bay leaf
½ large bunch of dill, fronds chopped
salt and pepper

Place a large stockpot over a medium–high heat and melt half the butter. Roughly chop the larger pieces of chicken, like the thighs and breasts – the drumsticks and wings can go in whole. Add the chicken pieces to the pot and cook on each side for 3–4 minutes or until the skin is golden (adjust the heat if it's too hot). Transfer the chicken to a plate. Add the remaining butter and the onion. Cook the onion for 7 minutes or until golden and translucent, adjusting the heat as needed. Add the carrots and cook, stirring occasionally, for 5 minutes.

Return the chicken to the pot, along with the potatoes, bay leaf, a generous amount of salt and pepper and enough water to cover the ingredients (a bit less than three-quarters of the pot). Cover with a lid, bring to a low–medium simmer and cook for 20 minutes, stirring occasionally.

Stir in the extra knob of butter and the dill. Put the lid back on and let stand, off the heat, for 15 minutes. Taste, adjust the seasoning and serve.

Savoury & Comforting

Slow-cooked Brisket with Prunes

Myaso s chernoslivom

I love to slow-cook this on a Sunday, ready for the week ahead. My babushka Liana often pairs meat with prunes, a common combination influenced by the Yiddish community that lived in Ukraine. Use any sort of beef or bone stock; I have made this plenty of times with just water. You could also use sweet paprika instead of mustard in this recipe. Serve with potatoes, boiled, baked, mashed with soured cream… however you wish.

SERVES 6-8

50g (1¾oz) butter or oil
1 onion, finely chopped
1 garlic clove, crushed
1 large carrot, thinly sliced into
    half-moons or quarters
1kg (2lb 4oz) brisket, diced into
    2cm (¾in) chunks
400g (14oz) passata
500ml (17fl oz) beef or bone stock
150g (5½oz) pitted prunes
1 Tbsp smooth or grainy mustard
1 bay leaf
salt and pepper
boiled, baked or mashed (I like this
    with soured cream mashed into
    the potatoes), to serve

Melt 30g (1oz) of the butter in a large casserole dish over a medium–high heat. Add the onion, garlic and carrot, then cook, stirring occasionally, for 5 minutes until slightly golden and aromatic. Take care not to burn the garlic – adjust the heat as needed. Remove the mixture from the dish.

Add the remaining butter to the dish and the diced brisket. Cook the meat on all sides over a medium–high heat for 10 minutes, then return the vegetable mixture. Stir in the passata, stock, prunes, mustard, bay leaf and 750ml (26fl oz) of water. Cover with a lid and gently simmer for 2½–3 hours over a low–medium heat. Check regularly, and if the liquid is evaporating too much, add another 250ml (9fl oz) of water.

After about 3 hours, remove from the heat, taste and season with salt and pepper. You can keep the meat chunky or use a fork to break it up.

Serve with boiled, baked or mashed potatoes, as you like.

Rice with Lamb and Barberries

Plov

Commonly served at market stalls and in the homes of Uzbekistan and other central Asian countries, plov travelled during the Soviet Union era. Every household has a slightly different recipe but generally plov has a core combination of rice, lamb, carrot matchsticks, onions, and an entire garlic bulb placed in the centre. The amount of fat or cooking oil might seem a lot, but much of it is absorbed by the rice.

SERVES 6-8

200g (7oz) fat (butter, ghee, sunflower or other vegetable oil, lamb tallow or a combination)

3 onions, roughly chopped

1kg (2lb 4oz) different cuts of lamb – ribs, diced leg and shoulder for best flavour and fat (keep the meat fairly chunky)

4 large carrots, sliced into thickish matchsticks about 3cm (1¼in) long

600g (1lb 5oz) basmati rice

1 whole garlic bulb

800ml (28fl oz) boiling water

20g (¾oz) dried barberries

salt and pepper

Place a large, lidded heavy-based casserole over a medium heat and melt the butter or fat. Add the onions and cook over a medium–high heat for 15 minutes, stirring occasionally. You want the onions to soften, become golden and almost melt into the fat, but not become dark or crunchy – adjust the heat accordingly.

Turn the heat to high and add the meat, stirring occasionally for 10–15 minutes. Then add 500ml (17fl oz) of water and a few pinches of salt and pepper. Cover with a lid, reduce the heat to low–medium and cook for about 30 minutes.

Remove the lid, increase the heat to medium–high and stir in the carrots. Cook for 10 minutes, stirring occasionally. Once the carrots have softened, season generously with salt, add the rice, garlic bulb and the boiling water – it needs to cover the surface of the rice by 1cm (½in). Bring up to a simmer over a high heat – you should see the rice rise to the surface. Cover with a lid. Reduce the heat to the lowest setting and cook for 45 minutes to an hour, then turn off the heat.

Once off the heat, wrap the lid in a kitchen towel or a muslin cloth (cheesecloth) and tie it around the handle. Place on top of the pan to cover it, and rest the plov for 15 minutes before serving and scattering over the barberries. The steam will be absorbed by the kitchen towel – so it reduces any condensation that might make the rice soggy.

Serve with cucumber slices and green tea, if you like.

Savoury & Comforting

Savoury & Comforting

Potato Pancakes
with Pork Filling
Kolduny

For these stuffed pancakes, try to buy pork mince with a really high fat content or make your own using high-quality pork belly which has a good meat-to-fat ratio. There are a lot of potatoes to grate here, but if you have a food processor with a grater attachment, it does the job in minutes. Enjoy with soured cream or the Aubergine Ikra (page 160).

SERVES 4 (MAKES ABOUT 10)

2kg (4lb 8oz) potatoes, peeled and
   rinsed, but left whole
3 Tbsp plain (all-purpose) flour
1 egg
500g (1lb 2oz) minced (ground) pork
¼ onion, finely diced
salt and pepper, to taste
4 Tbsp water
butter or oil, for cooking
soured cream, to serve

Coarsely grate the potatoes, then tip into a bowl with the flour and egg and mix well to combine. In a separate bowl, thoroughly mix together the pork, onion, salt, pepper and the water for 5 minutes.

Put about 3 tablespoons of the potato mixture into the palm of your hand and flatten it to about 1cm (½in) thick. Fill with about 1 heaped tablespoon of the pork filling. Press the sides inwards to make an oval patty shape, adding more potato to cover the filling as needed. Repeat to make about ten.

Preheat the oven to 180°C fan/200°C/400°F/Gas mark 6. Meanwhile, place a large frying pan over a medium–high heat and add a knob of butter or a glug of oil. Cook the kolduny in batches, a few at a time, for 6 minutes on each side or until golden brown. At this point, transfer them to a cast-iron dish or medium, deep-sided baking tray. Place them side by side, so they are touching, but not on top of each other. Cover with a lid or foil and place in the oven for 25–30 minutes. Serve straight away with soured cream.

Potato and Pork Babka
Bulbianaja babka

Normally, this savoury babka is made with cured pork fat (salo, see page 12), but pancetta is an option; as it has a stronger flavour, you can use less. To make this vegetarian, cook chopped mushrooms in butter and add these to the mixture in place of the meat.

SERVES 2–4

100g (3½oz) thinly sliced salo
(or use pancetta)
1 onion, finely chopped
1kg (2lb 4oz) potatoes, peeled and
rinsed, but left whole
1 egg
1 Tbsp plain (all-purpose) flour
2 Tbsp breadcrumbs
salt and pepper
soured cream, to serve (optional)

Preheat the oven to 180°C fan/200°C/400°F/Gas mark 6. Heat a large cast-iron frying pan over a medium–high heat and pan-fry the salo for about 2 minutes. Add the onion and cook for about 8–10 minutes until softened, golden and slightly crispy. Transfer to a large mixing bowl and leave to cool slightly. Set aside the cast-iron pan to use later.

Coarsely grate the potatoes – use a food processor with a grater attachment, if you have one. Add the potatoes to the onion bowl, along with the egg, flour and some salt and pepper. Mix everything together.

Coat the base of the frying pan with the breadcrumbs, using the residual fat to help stick the crumbs to the surface – or lightly oil a baking tray if your pan is not ovenproof. Transfer the potato mixture to the cast-iron pan, spread out evenly and pat down well. Transfer to the oven and cook for 45 minutes.

Serve hot from the oven, with soured cream if you like.

Kefir Pie,
Two ways

Piroh z zielianinaj /
Piroh z kapustaj

My late babushka Lida and I made this *piroh*, or *pierog* (pie) for her 80th birthday in her small kitchen back in Baranavichy, Belarus. The dough is made with kefir, soured cream, and lots of butter, resulting in a deliciously rich pastry. The mixed greens and cheese filling is incredibly moreish, but I love the cabbage filling just as much. This pie is usually eaten cooled, either a few hours after it is cooked or the following day, but if you can't wait, enjoy it fresh out of the oven.

For the dough

600g (1lb 5oz) plain (all-purpose) flour, plus extra for dusting

250g (9oz) cold butter, plus extra for greasing

2 generous pinches of salt

250ml (9fl oz) kefir (for homemade see page 148, or use store-bought)

125ml (4fl oz) soured cream

½ tsp bicarbonate of soda (baking soda)

1 tsp apple cider vinegar

egg wash (1 small egg beaten with a dash of milk)

your choice of filling (see opposite and overleaf)

Sift the flour into a large mixing bowl and coarsely grate the butter directly into the bowl. Toss the butter through the flour with your fingers to a rough breadcrumb consistency, then mix in the salt. In a separate bowl, whisk together the kefir and soured cream, then add this to the flour mixture. In a small cup mix together the bicarbonate of soda and vinegar and, when fizzing, add to the mixture too.

Combine and knead the dough for about 3 minutes using your hands (or you can use a stand mixer fitted with a dough hook and knead by hand for the last few minutes). Bring it together into a smooth ball and place in a lightly oiled bowl, cover with a plate or cling film (plastic wrap) and place in the refrigerator for 30 minutes.

Meanwhile, make your chosen filling.

When you are ready to cook, preheat the oven to 180°C fan/ 200°C/400°F/Gas mark 6, and grease a 24 x 30cm (9½ x 12in) baking tray with butter.

To assemble the pie, generously flour a work surface. Cut the chilled dough into two, one piece a little larger than the other. Roll out the larger piece first, slightly bigger than the baking tray: you want the pastry to slightly overlap the sides by about 1cm (½in). Both the base and lid of the pie should be around 2–3mm (1/16–1/10in) thick.

Savoury & Comforting

Fill the pie following the instructions below and overleaf, depending on which filling you choose.

Roll out the smaller piece of pastry, big enough to top the pie. Transfer it onto the tray and press tightly onto the pastry edges. Finish by pressing them together with a fork and pierce holes in the surface for the steam to escape. Brush all over with the egg wash.

Place on the lower shelf of the oven and cook for 1 hour until the pastry is golden. Leave to cool in the tray for at least 30 minutes before serving, otherwise cool entirely, cover with a clean towel and serve at room temperature.

FOR THE CABBAGE, CARROT AND CARAWAY FILLING

30g (1oz) cold butter, diced, for topping, plus extra for cooking
1 onion, finely sliced into half-moons
½ large cabbage, stem removed, shredded or finely sliced
1 carrot, grated
½ tsp caraway seeds
100g (3½oz) sauerkraut (or use 2 Tbsp apple cider vinegar)
salt and pepper

Heat a large frying pan over a medium–high heat and add a generous amount of butter. Add the onion and sauté for 5–7 minutes, stirring occasionally, until softened. Add the cabbage and 2–3 pinches of salt. Cook for 20 minutes over a medium–high heat, stirring every few minutes. Mix through the carrot, caraway seeds and sauerkraut. Cook for another 10–15 minutes or until everything has softened and reduced; the cabbage should have cooked through and darkened in colour. Taste and season with salt and pepper: it should be soft, sweet, salty and aromatic. Remove from the heat and transfer to a bowl to cool.

Add the filling to the pie, topped with the diced butter.

FOR THE GREENS, EGG AND CHEESE FILLING

5 eggs
150g (5½oz) spring onions (scallions)
  – about half a bunch, washed
  and trimmed
80g (2¾oz) dill (roughly half a bunch),
  thick stems removed
110g (3¾oz) parsley (roughly half a
  bunch), thick stems removed
300g (10½oz) bryndza or feta, crumbled
280g (10oz) havarti or cream cheese,
  broken into smaller pieces
200g (7oz) aged mozzarella (melting
  mozzarella) or sulguni, grated
30g (1oz) cold butter, diced, for topping
salt

Put the eggs into a saucepan of cold water, bring to a simmer and cook for 9 minutes. Drain, then refill the pan with cold water and leave until cool. Peel and slice the eggs and set aside.

Place the spring onions and herbs on a board and very finely slice. Add to a large mixing bowl, season with a small pinch of salt and mix together thoroughly.

Layer up the pie with your prepared ingredients: first the mixed greens, then the cheeses, then the sliced eggs and finally with the diced butter.

Pictured opposite.

HOMEMADE KEFIR

My mum often makes kefir (cultured milk) from scratch at home. It's incredibly simple and such a staple. You just need to buy some kefir grains, available online (see page 201). I always use kefir in doughs, soups and desserts, as well as smoothies for my daughter. At home we often drink it in the mornings as it is.

MAKES ABOUT 500ML (17FL OZ)

1 heaped Tbsp kefir grains
250ml (9fl oz) full-fat (whole)
  milk (preferably organic and
  unhomogenized)

Place the kefir grains into a large jar with the milk. Cover with a muslin cloth (cheesecloth) and let it stand for 24 hours or so. If the room is cold, it may take longer.

Strain the kefir off the grains and drink straight away, or store in the refrigerator for up to a week. Continue to reuse the kefir grains by transferring them to a new jar with fresh milk each time. If stored correctly, they will last a very long time – check the packaging for instructions on safe storage.

Savoury & Comforting

Celebrations

Celebrations

Recipes for special occasions
& gatherings

Some of my best memories are of getting together for a memorable feast, often to celebrate an important moment in life. All you need is good food, great company and a place to gather. It's a chance to bring out tablecloths, cutlery and glassware used only for celebrations, to make it feel special.

When I was growing up, Mum would ask me to help set out the food she'd been preparing, often for days, on long tables. To start, there would be ice-cold vodka and plates of *zakusky* (small bites or appetizers) – beetroot-cured gravlax, fresh bread slathered with chicken pâté or salmon caviar, or salted herring with raw slices of onion and rye bread – alongside salads and dips, devilled eggs, pickles, aubergine rolls. If all that wasn't enough, she would serve a main dish, such as roast duck with plums and apples stuffed with buckwheat, or salmon baked in a herb crust with boiled potatoes topped with butter or soured cream.

These are the recipes we turn to for special occasions, taken from moments I've shared at my home in Sydney and from ones I treasure from visits to Belarus and Ukraine. Look to this chapter when you are feeding a crowd.

Ice-cold Vodka and Zakusky

Ledyanaya vodka i zakusky

If you plan to serve vodka at your next gathering, put the bottle in the freezer the day before so that when you take it out, the vodka is ice cold.

My parents taught me how to drink vodka – responsibly, I should say – by watching their many gatherings with friends both in Sydney and back in Ukraine and Belarus. A shot of vodka, accompanied by appetizers, or zakusky, would always be drunk after a memorable toast, long or short: the first is usually to the occasion; the second (very shortly afterwards) to friendship and to everyone sharing the occasion; the third is a toast to love or to the parents; the fourth and so on are to the women, men... and the rest can get quite philosophical, sometimes emotional, so bring tissues! I can never get past four shots, so don't push it if you ever find yourself at the table with Eastern Europeans – just enjoy the food.

Zakusky tend to be cold, and either very salty or fatty or strongly flavoured – usually something garlicky or with a kick from grated raw horseradish or mustard. Here are some simple pairings that are easily put together. Enjoy with freshly sliced rye bread.

ZAKUSKY SUGGESTIONS:
- Butter, salmon fish roe or black caviar
- Butter and thickly cut salami slices
- Salo with a bit of mustard
- Salo made into a paste with crushed raw garlic and salt
- Sliced herring or salted and freshly cured mackerel with raw onion
- Tvorog mixed with chopped spring onions (scallions), radishes and salt
- Raw tomatoes sliced in half and filled with egg, cheese and black pepper
- Platter of mixed vegetable pickles and ferments, particularly pickled mushrooms (see page 76) and raw onion
- Slow-cooked ox tongue with horseradish

Chicken Pâté and Pickles

Kurinyy pashtet i solenyye ogurtsy

We nearly always have this pâté as part of the spread for our family celebrations. I've added a guide below for how much butter to use, but the amount does depend on the chicken livers. Serve with bread and some salty gherkins or other pickles. *Pictured on page 153.*

MAKES 2 x 250ML (9OZ) RAMEKINS

60g (2¼oz) butter for cooking,
  plus an extra 50–80g (1¾–2¾oz)
  softened, for blending, plus 50g
  (1¾oz) for covering the surface
½ onion, chopped
1 carrot, grated
500g (1lb 2oz) chicken livers, pieces
  whole but membranes trimmed
a few sage leaves, chopped
1 garlic clove, crushed
salt and pepper

To serve
sliced bread or sourdough baguette
pickled gherkins or cucumbers (see
  page 66 for homemade)

Heat a large frying pan over a medium–high heat and add 30g (1oz) of the butter for cooking and the onion. Fry for 7–10 minutes until soft and golden. Add the carrot and cook for a further 5 minutes. Scrape the onion and carrot into a small bowl and set aside.

Add the remaining 30g (1oz) of butter to the pan and place back over a medium heat. Cook the liver pieces for about 10–15 minutes, turning them over halfway through (don't overcook: you want them soft and moist in the centre, so adjust the heat as needed). In the last 2 minutes of cooking the liver, add the sage and garlic, along with the cooked carrot and onion. Stir and season with salt and pepper. Add a small splash (1–2 tablespoons) of hot water, turn off the heat and cover with a lid to keep the liver soft. Let it sit for 5 minutes.

While it's still warm, transfer the mixture to a food processor and add 50g (1¾oz) of the softened butter. Blend for a few minutes until the texture is smooth. Taste and adjust the seasoning, adding a splash more hot water or extra softened butter if the mixture needs it. If you want a creamier consistency, pass the mixture through a sieve.

Divide between ramekins, levelling the surface with the back of a spoon. Melt the remaining 50g (1¾oz) of butter and pour over the ramekins to cover the surface evenly. Place in the refrigerator for at least 1 hour or until the pâté is cold and the butter has solidified. It will keep, covered, for up to a week in the refrigerator like this.

Serve on slices of toast or bread, topped with pickles.

Celebrations

Devilled Eggs

Farshirovannyye yaytsa

This Eastern European twist on devilled eggs is a staple in almost every zakusky spread. They are so moreish and well-seasoned, with a garlicky creamy filling – perfect with a shot of ice-cold vodka. Use more or less cheese if you wish. *Pictured on page 153.*

SERVES 5 AS AN APPETIZER

10 large eggs
2 Tbsp mayonnaise
1 garlic clove, crushed
1 tsp mustard
40g (1½oz) mature (sharp) cheddar, finely grated
½ bunch of chives, chopped
¼ bunch of dill, fronds chopped
salt and pepper

Place the eggs in a large saucepan of water. Cover with a lid and bring to the boil. Once boiling, cook for 9 minutes. Pour away the hot water, refill with cold water and leave the eggs for 5 minutes.

Peel the eggs and slice in half lengthways. Scoop the yolks into a bowl and mash with a fork. Add the mayonnaise, garlic, mustard and cheese and season with salt and pepper. Mix to combine, then use a teaspoon to fill the egg halves (or pipe the mixture in). Sprinkle the herbs over the top.

Beetroot and Vodka-cured Salmon Gravlax with Blini

Malosol'nyy losos' s blinami

This cured salmon can be prepared ahead of time, making it a convenient dish when cooking for a crowd – and it looks beautiful, too. If you can, go to your local fishmonger for the freshest salmon you can find and ask for the fillet to be pin-boned. You can also use the curing mixture here for other oily fish, such as trout.

MAKES 32–36 BITE-SIZED BLINI

1.5kg (3lb 5oz) skin-on salmon fillet, pin-boned

For the cure
4 large beetroots, washed and grated (no need to peel)
zest of 3 lemons
1 Tbsp juniper berries, crushed in a pestle and mortar
300g (10½oz) sea salt flakes
150g (5½oz) brown sugar
2 Tbsp vodka

For the blini
1 x quantity Eastern European Pancakes batter (page 21)

To serve
200–250ml (7–9fl oz) soured cream
½ red onion, finely diced
small bunch of dill, fronds chopped
salmon fish roe (red caviar), optional

First prepare the curing mixture. Put the grated beetroot and any liquid in a large bowl with the lemon zest, juniper berries, salt, sugar and the vodka. Mix together.

To make the gravlax, cover the base of a large, deep-sided baking tray (slightly longer and a few centimetres wider than your piece of salmon) with 4 long, overlapping layers of cling film (plastic wrap), allowing them to generously overlap on all sides. Spread a layer of the beetroot mixture on top of the cling film, making it slightly wider and longer than the salmon itself. Place the salmon, skin-side down, on top, then cover it with the rest of the beetroot cure, completely encasing it. Fold the edges of the cling film over the salmon to wrap it entirely. Cover the tray with another layer of film and transfer it to the refrigerator. Leave the salmon to cure for 24–36 hours.

When you are ready to serve, remove the wrapping, scrape off the beetroot cure and pat the salmon dry with paper towels. Keep the salmon refrigerated.

Meanwhile, make 16–18 blini following the method on page 21.

To assemble, slice the blini in half, then fold in half again to make 32–36 triangles. Slice the salmon thinly with a sharp knife (remove the skin as you go; I find keeping the skin on makes it easier to slice thinly). Top the folded blini with a teaspoon of soured cream, a slice of gravlax, some diced onion, dill and ½ teaspoon of salmon fish roe.

Celebrations

Rye Bread, Topped Three Ways

Otkrytyye buterbrody

If you ever find yourself at a celebration dinner at my family's house, there will always be a selection of dips ready to eat on the table. Most likely the three I've shared here. Serve these with plenty of fresh or toasted rye bread for sharing.

SERVES 6–8 AS AN APPETIZER

4 medium to large beetroots, washed, unpeeled
1 garlic clove, crushed unless roasting with the beetroot
sunflower oil
handful of walnuts, roughly chopped
100g (3½oz) pitted prunes, roughly chopped
2 Tbsp mayonnaise (optional)
salt

BEETROOT, PRUNE AND WALNUT SALAD | *SALAT IZ SVEKLY*

Walnuts and prunes are a classic addition to beetroot in Eastern Europe. Do add raw garlic if you like strong flavours, or roast it whole along with the beets for a sweeter, gentler flavour.

Preheat the oven to 180°C fan/200°C/400°F/Gas mark 6. Place the beetroots, and the garlic if roasting, in an ovenproof dish, with a splash of water at the bottom. Sprinkle with salt and drizzle with oil. Roast for about 1 hour, removing the garlic after 20 minutes. Check with a skewer that the largest beetroot is completely cooked – if soft in the centre, it's ready. Set aside to cool completely.

Remove the skins from the cooled beetroots (it should come off easily just by using your hands; otherwise you can do it under cool running water). Grate the beetroots coarsely into a medium mixing bowl. Add the crushed or roasted garlic, walnuts and prunes, and season with salt. If you're using mayonnaise add it at this point too. Stir through, taste and adjust the seasoning.

SERVES 6–8 AS AN APPETIZER

2 large aubergines (eggplants)
1 small onion, halved
1–2 red (bell) peppers
3 large garlic cloves
2 red chillies (optional)
sunflower oil
350ml (12fl oz) passata or canned
   chopped tomatoes
salt and pepper
handful of parsley, roughly chopped

BABUSHKA LIANA'S AUBERGINE IKRA | *BAKLAZHANNA IKRA*

Don't ask me why but 'ikra' translates as 'caviar' in English. Babushka Liana nearly always has a few jars of this in the refrigerator, and for good reason. She grew an abundance of aubergines and courgettes in her garden outside Kharkiv, so she has many recipes that make the most of a glut. Ikra can be made with either – just replace the two aubergines with four courgettes (zucchini). In summer I like to cook the vegetables over a fire outside for a lovely smoky flavour. This is delicious with shashlyk (Lamb Skewers, page 108) and kotleti (Stuffed Chicken Rissoles, page 168). Babushka Liana also recommends adding a spoonful of adjika (Fermented Pepper Sauce, page 78), along with the passata, if you have any.

Preheat the oven to 210°C fan/230°C/450°F/Gas mark 8. Place the aubergines on a large baking tray and pierce the skins using a fork. Add the onion halves to the tray along with the whole red peppers, garlic and chillies (if using). Season generously with salt and drizzle with plenty of oil, then cook for 40 minutes. After 20 minutes remove the garlic, then after 30 minutes remove the onion, peppers and chillies.

Once ready, remove the aubergines from the oven. Leave the ingredients to cool. Slice the aubergines in half, scoop out the soft flesh and roughly chop on a board. Remove the skin and seeds from the red peppers and roughly chop the flesh. Chop the onion, garlic and chillies too. Mix everything together with a fork or blitz in a food processor for a smoother consistency.

Heat a large frying pan over a medium heat and add a generous drizzle of sunflower oil to cover the base of the pan. Transfer the aubergine mixture to the pan, add the passata and some salt and pepper and cook for about 15 minutes, stirring often. Taste and adjust the seasoning. Turn off the heat and add the chopped parsley. Cool and store in a jar or container in the refrigerator for up to a week.

Pictured on page 159.

Celebrations

SERVES 6 AS AN APPETIZER

30g (1oz) butter
½ onion, finely diced
700g (1lb 9oz) mushrooms, washed
  or brushed and roughly chopped
a few thyme sprigs
pinch of paprika, sweet or smoked
1 heaped Tbsp mayonnaise
  or soured cream
salt and pepper

MUSHROOM IKRA | *HRYBNAJA IKRA*

Fried mushrooms of any sort are delicious, and this recipe couldn't be more simple. I recommend using seasonal mushrooms sourcing different varieties. Any sort of brown mushrooms, chanterelles or porcini will do. For a stronger flavour, rub toasted rye bread with a clove of raw garlic before topping.

Heat a large frying pan over a medium–high heat, add the butter and onion, and cook for 7–10 minutes or until golden and softened. Add the mushrooms and cook down, stirring, for 10 minutes. Once the water from the mushrooms has evaporated, add the thyme, paprika and a good seasoning of salt and pepper. Stir, cooking for a further 7–10 minutes or until the mushrooms have shrunk in size and have started to catch, showing a bit of golden colour.

Transfer to a bowl, cool for 5 minutes, then stir through the mayonnaise or soured cream. Serve straight away or store in the refrigerator until ready to serve.

Pictured on page 159.

Tvorog-stuffed Aubergine Rolls

Ruletyky z baklazhaniv

These light, herby aubergine rolls are great for sharing. If you're using tvorog that comes with a bit of liquid, place the cheese into a muslin/ cheesecloth-lined sieve and squeeze to remove the excess liquid. This moreish recipe also works nicely with other soft, tangy white cheeses, such as quark or a soft curd cheese.

SERVES 4–6 AS AN APPETIZER

sunflower oil, for frying
2 medium or large aubergines
   (eggplants), thinly sliced lengthways
500g (1lb 2oz) tvorog or cottage cheese
½ bunch of parsley, leaves finely
   chopped (reserve a few whole
   to garnish)
½ bunch of dill, fronds finely chopped
   (reserve a few fronds to garnish)
zest and juice of 1 lemon
chilli flakes (optional)
2 handfuls of walnuts, roughly chopped
salt

Pour a generous amount of oil into a large frying pan over a medium–high heat. Add as many aubergine slices as will fit in a single layer and cook for about 3 minutes on each side. Aubergine absorbs a lot of oil so you will need to add more as you cook the rest. Season with salt on each side and place the cooked slices on a plate lined with paper towels while you cook the rest. Set aside to cool.

Meanwhile, make the filling. Put the tvorog and chopped herbs in a food processor and whip until blended and green – or simply mix together in a bowl. Add the lemon zest, juice and chilli flakes (if using) and season with salt. Whip again until smooth. Taste and adjust the seasoning.

Lay the aubergine slices on a board, place a tablespoon of filling on one end of each slice and roll up. Arrange on a plate, sprinkle with the walnuts and top with the herbs. Serve immediately.

Layered Beetroot, Potato and Herring Salad

Silodka pod shuboy

This traditional dish is affectionately known as 'herring under a fur coat', though I like to describe it as a 'salad cake' due to its many layers, including grated beetroot, potatoes and salted herring. It's often served for special celebrations, including New Year's Eve, and usually made in large quantities so that it can also be enjoyed for a recovery breakfast the next day.

The herring is best sourced from an Eastern European deli. If you want to make this vegetarian, you can replace the herring with 250g (9oz) walnuts. This is best made in advance as, once assembled, it needs time to rest.

SERVES 6–8

5 medium beetroots, washed, unpeeled
4 medium potatoes, washed and peeled
3 medium carrots, washed and peeled
3 large eggs
250g (9oz) mayonnaise
200ml (7fl oz) soured cream
250g (9oz) herring, diced small
1 large green apple, peeled and cored
a few parsley sprigs
salt

Preheat the oven to 180°C fan/200°C/400°F/Gas mark 6. Place the beetroots on a baking tray and roast for about 50–60 minutes. Check with a skewer that the largest beetroot is completely cooked – if soft in the centre, it's ready. Set aside to cool completely.

Meanwhile, put the potatoes and carrots in a large saucepan with enough water to cover. Bring to a simmer and cook over a medium heat for about 15 minutes until cooked through to the centre – be careful not to overcook them. Drain and set aside to cool. Put the eggs in a separate saucepan of water. Cover with a lid and bring to the boil. Once boiling, cook for 9 minutes. Drain the hot water, refill with cold water and leave the eggs for 5 minutes.

Peel and coarsely grate the potatoes and carrots, keeping them separate. Peel and finely grate the eggs, setting aside one of the grated egg yolks and whites for use as garnish. Peel and coarsely grate the beetroots, then divide the mixture in half. Place one half between layers of paper towel, squeeze the juice from it and repeat with the second half. In a bowl mix the mayonnaise together with the soured cream.

To assemble, select a large flat dinner plate. Spread the diced herring over the plate, then layer with the grated potatoes and a sprinkle of salt. Spread about 4–5 tablespoons of the mayo mixture over the potatoes, pressing down with a fork and piercing some holes to help the mayo soak into the ingredients underneath. Next, spread the grated carrot over the top and sprinkle with salt. Grate over the apple to form another layer. Spread another 4–5 tablespoons of the mayo mixture on top. Use a fork again to pierce some holes. Spread the grated eggs over, another sprinkle of salt, then the grated beetroot, another sprinkle of salt and finally the rest of the mayo mixture. Use the back of a spoon to help smooth it into a dome-like shape. Top with the reserved grated egg white and yolk.

Leave to rest on the worktop for 1 hour, then transfer into the refrigerator to rest for a few more hours before serving.

Mushroom Cheese Bake

Gribnoy julienne

This warming dish is great for sharing during autumn or winter – enjoy
it straight from the pan with fresh crusty bread for dipping. To make this
more substantial, serve with potatoes on the side. I like to include a variety
of mushrooms for this. Use a cheese such as a light cheddar or another
melting cheese.

SERVES 4 AS AN APPETIZER

70g (2½oz) butter
¼ onion, diced
2 garlic cloves, crushed
500g (1lb 2oz) mushrooms
　　(white, button, chestnut/Swiss are
　　all suitable, or a mixture), washed
　　or brushed then roughly chopped
3 heaped Tbsp soured cream
2 Tbsp plain (all-purpose) flour
60g (2¼oz) light cheddar cheese,
　　havarti or other melting cheese
　　such as firm mozzarella, grated
salt and pepper

Preheat the oven to 180°C fan/200°C/400°F/Gas mark 6. Heat
an ovenproof cast-iron pan over a medium–high heat and add
20g (¾oz) of the butter. Once the butter is melted, add the
onion and cook, stirring, for 7 minutes. Add the garlic and cook
for a further 3 minutes (reduce the heat if it's too hot – you
don't want the garlic to burn). Set the onion and garlic aside
until needed.

Add the remaining 50g (1¾oz) of butter to the pan with the
mushrooms and cook, stirring, for 5 minutes until they soften.
The mushrooms will release water at this stage. Return the
onion and garlic to the pan and season generously with salt
and pepper. Stir in the soured cream and flour and mix well.

Remove from the heat, top with grated cheese and place in
the oven for 20 minutes or until the cheese has melted and is
golden and crispy in parts.

Tip: If you don't have a cast-iron pan, you can prepare the
mixture in any type of pan and then transfer it to a baking dish
before moving to the oven.

Stuffed Chicken Rissoles

Farshirovannyye kotleti

Serve these fresh so that when you cut into them the buttery mushroom filling is soft and runny. I love to eat these with a platter of the freshest possible vegetables – radishes, tomatoes, cucumbers, spring onions – all with a very generous sprinkle of salt, and warm potatoes topped with lots of dill and butter or, if you have it, golden unrefined sunflower oil.

SERVES 4–6 (MAKES ABOUT 12)

2 small onions, very finely chopped
1kg (2lb 4oz) minced (ground) chicken
100g (3½oz) butter or sunflower oil for cooking, plus extra butter for the filling
550g (1lb 4oz) mushrooms, very finely diced
1 garlic clove, finely chopped
150g (5½oz) breadcrumbs
1kg (2lb 4oz) potatoes, washed, unpeeled
½ bunch of fresh dill, fronds chopped
salt and pepper
radishes, to serve

Set aside half the chopped onion. Transfer the other half to a bowl with the chicken, season well with salt and pepper and mix thoroughly.

Heat a large frying pan over a high heat and add 40g (1½oz) of the butter or oil along with the mushrooms and stir them through. The mushrooms will quickly absorb the fat. Let the mushrooms cook and release their liquid – this takes about 2 minutes – stirring them occasionally. Then, add the other half of the chopped onions and season with a pinch of salt. Cook, stirring, for a few minutes until the liquid has mostly evaporated. The mixture should smell earthy and aromatic. Stir through the garlic and turn off the heat – you want a bit of 'rawness' to the garlic. Transfer the mushrooms to a bowl and set aside until warm but not hot.

To make the stuffed chicken rissoles, place the breadcrumbs in a shallow bowl. Wet your hands and take around 90g (3½oz) of the raw chicken mixture. I recommend weighing the first amount so you get a good idea of the approximate amount you need. Flatten it in the palm of your hand to an oval shape about 1cm (½in) thick. Place 2 heaped teaspoons of the cooled mushroom mixture in the centre, then a small knob of butter (about a third of a teaspoon) on top. Bring the outside edges together, encasing the mushroom filling and covering any holes with extra chicken mince. Reshape your rissole into an oval and place in the bowl of breadcrumbs, coating on all sides. Set aside on a board and make the rest.

Heat a large pan over a medium–high heat and add a generous amount of butter (about 20g/¾oz) or about a tablespoon of oil. Once hot, add a few rissoles to the pan without overcrowding them. Cook for about 3½ minutes on each side or until the surfaces are golden and crispy, adjusting the heat as needed. Set aside the cooked rissoles and keep warm while you cook the next batch, adding more butter or oil to the pan between batches.

Meanwhile, put the potatoes in a medium–large pan and cover with water. Add a generous seasoning of salt. Cover with a lid and bring to a simmer. Move the lid slightly to the edge and simmer the potatoes for about 15 minutes. The time depends on the type and size of your potatoes, but I recommend checking the centre of one after about 15 minutes by piercing it with a fork. Once cooked, drain and transfer the potatoes to a serving bowl and add generous amounts of butter, salt and dill.

Serve the rissoles with the potatoes and radishes or other fresh vegetables of your liking.

Herb-crusted Salmon with Potatoes, Caviar and Cream

Losos' iz dukhovki

This herb-crusted salmon is a beautiful main for special occasions. I like to bring this to the table on a large platter or board and serve everyone at the table, as it looks so impressive fresh out of the oven. Adjust the herb ratio to your liking.

SERVES 6–8

1 large side of salmon (about 1.5kg/ 3lb 5oz), unskinned but scaled and deboned
1 bunch each of dill (60g/2¼oz), parsley (40g/1½oz), and tarragon (10g/¼oz), washed
1 bunch of spring onions (scallions) (50g/1¾oz), ends trimmed
80ml (2½fl oz) oil
1kg (2lb 4oz) baby potatoes, washed
salt and pepper

To serve
150ml (5fl oz) soured cream
salmon fish roe (red caviar)
2 spring onions (scallions), chopped
handful of dill

Preheat the oven to 180°C fan/200°C/400°F/Gas mark 6 and line a large baking tray with baking paper. Wash and pat dry the salmon side on paper towels. Place the salmon on the lined baking tray.

Remove any tough stems from the herbs. Put the herbs and spring onions in a food processor along with the oil and some salt and pepper. Blend to a fairly smooth paste. Coat the salmon with the paste, then smooth it out using the back of a spoon. Place in the oven and cook for 30–35 minutes or slightly longer, depending on the size of your salmon – check the centre using a fork to make sure it's cooked through.

Meanwhile put the potatoes in a saucepan and cover with water. Add a large pinch of salt. Bring to the boil and simmer for 10–15 minutes until just cooked. Check the potatoes by piercing one with a skewer; if it's soft in the centre, they are done. Drain the water and set the potatoes aside, covered with a lid, until the salmon is cooked.

To serve, transfer the salmon to a large board or serving platter, with the potatoes on the side. Top the potatoes with a small dollop of soured cream, ¼ teaspoon of fish roe (or however much you'd like), and the chopped spring onions and dill.

Celebrations

Roast Duck with Buckwheat, Plums and Apples

Utka v dukhovke

For special occasions in Eastern Europe, a whole duck, or the neck, is often stuffed with buckwheat and cooked with fruits. Here, I use apples and plums; though, if you're not roasting the duck with fruits, you could also enjoy it with a sour cherry sauce (see opposite). Use toasted buckwheat for the filling, which can be found in Eastern European delis.

SERVES 4

100g (3½oz) toasted buckwheat (kasha)
2kg (4lb 8oz) whole duck
60g (2¼oz) duck fat, melted
800g (1lb 12oz) potatoes (any), washed, unpeeled and halved lengthways
6 shallots, halved lengthways
7 plums, halved and pitted
4 apples, cored and halved or quartered
½ bunch each of dill and parsley, roughly chopped
1 garlic clove, crushed
2 Tbsp sunflower oil
salt and pepper

First prepare the buckwheat for the stuffing. Tip the toasted buckwheat into a medium saucepan and half-fill it with water. Bring to the boil. Once boiling, drain the buckwheat through a sieve, discarding the water. Return the buckwheat to the pan, add 250ml (9fl oz) of cold water and season with salt. Bring back to the boil, reduce to a simmer and cover with a lid. Cook at a low simmer for about 10–15 minutes or until almost all the water has been absorbed. Remove from the heat and set aside, uncovered, to cool.

Preheat the oven to 200°C fan/220°C/425°F/Gas mark 7. Pat the duck skin dry with a paper towel and place on a large baking tray. Mix the cooled buckwheat with salt and pepper. Use your hands or a large spoon to fill the cavity of the duck with the mixture. Pour half the melted fat over the duck, then transfer to the oven and roast for 45 minutes.

After 45 minutes, take the tray from the oven and arrange the potatoes, shallots, plums and apples around the duck. Pour over the rest of the duck fat, basting the duck itself, and season well with salt and pepper. Return to the oven and reduce the heat to 190°C fan/210°C/410°F/Gas mark 6½. Cook for another 50 minutes or so (see tips, opposite).

Mix the herbs, garlic and oil in a small bowl and season with salt and pepper. Serve the duck and all the trimmings on a serving platter topped with the garlicky herbs.

250g (9oz) frozen pitted sour cherries
1 tsp ground cinnamon
½ tsp nutmeg
2 heaped Tbsp honey
1 heaped tsp brown sugar
1 Tbsp cornflour (cornstarch)
    or potato starch
salt

VARIATION: SOUR CHERRY SAUCE

Put the cherries, spices, honey, sugar and a pinch of salt into a small saucepan and bring to a simmer. Add the cornflour and stir through well. Simmer for 10 minutes, stirring occasionally. Spoon over the duck to serve.

Tips: A duck weighing around 2kg (4lb 8oz) roasts in about 1½ hours. Give it an extra 15–30 minutes in the oven if it's bigger. How to tell when the duck is ready? The skin will be dark, golden and crispy. The legs will feel loose when you move them. If you pierce the thickest part of the thigh with a skewer, the juices that run out should be clear.

Sweet & Indulgent

Sweet & Indulgent

Recipes for sweet occasions

There is this one vivid memory that I have of my 5-year-old self, sitting at a long table in our apartment in Kharkiv, on Lermontovskaya Street. I was watching a plateful of sweets being placed on the table. Steaming-hot black tea was being served from a *samovar*. There was a little crystal glass bowl containing sugar cubes and a box of chocolate-coated prunes soaked in cognac or some sort of alcohol that someone had brought over. I quickly tried one of those prune chocolates before anyone could stop me, immediately regretting it but finding relief in the tea and the sugar cubes as I crunched on them. I often think about why such a seemingly small moment is one of my enduring memories from Ukraine. Perhaps it was my conscious discovery of sugar.

From yeasted bakes, slowly cooked cakes and honeyed-up layers of pastry to cinnamon-spiced and sweetened tvorog, syrupy sour cherries, luscious creams, silky custards and soured-cream-enriched doughs – these are the recipes of my childhood.

Chocolate Cheesecake 'House'

Šakaladny tvarožnik domik

This chocolate cheesecake, shaped like the roof of a house, is often made the day before a special occasion. This was always my favourite time to watch my mum in the kitchen – the surfaces laden with ingredients, pots bubbling on the stove and delicious smells in the air.

MAKES 10–12 SLICES

For the filling
700g (1lb 9oz) tvorog or cottage cheese, left out the refrigerator for 30 minutes before using – use a drier-style tvorog for best results
50g (1¾oz) icing (confectioner's) sugar, sifted
70g (2½oz) unsalted butter, softened

For the chocolate layer
80g (2¾oz) cacao
100g (3½oz) icing (confectioner's) sugar
300g (10½oz) unsalted butter, softened
1 tsp almond liqueur (optional – for alcohol-free, replace with 1 tsp ground cinnamon)

For the 'house'
27 rectangular milk biscuits (cookies) – we use the Arnott's brand but any rectangular-shaped ones will do
125ml (4fl oz) lukewarm milk

Leave the tvorog to sit in a muslin-lined sieve and squeeze out any excess liquid before using. For the filling, add the icing sugar to a large bowl with the tvorog and mix with a fork. In a separate bowl, mash the butter with a spoonful of the tvorog mixture, then transfer to the large bowl, mix and set aside.

To make the chocolate layer, sift the cacao and icing sugar into a bowl and mix to combine. Put the softened butter in another bowl, add the dry ingredients and the almond liqueur or cinnamon and use a fork to mix together.

To assemble the 'house', double-line a 50cm (20in) long wooden board (ensure it fits in your refrigerator) with a large sheet of foil and baking paper. Use a spatula to spread the cacao mixture on the base of the baking paper to form a rectangle roughly the width of three of your biscuits and the length of nine of them. (Lay out the biscuits first as a guide: the chocolate coating can be spread a touch wider.)

Working quickly, dip the biscuits one at a time into the warm milk (they will expand a little), and place them on the chocolate, three in a row, with their longer sides along the shorter edge of the chocolate. Continue with the remaining biscuits to make nine rows, covering the chocolate and topping with the cheese mixture, smoothing out the surface.

Lift under the baking paper to turn the long edge inwards, joining it to the opposite edge to make a long, triangular roof shape. Smooth out the chocolate to fill any gaps. Wrap the *domik* tightly with the baking paper and foil, twisting the edges of the paper and foil together like a Christmas cracker. Refrigerate overnight. The next day, unwrap, slice and serve.

Sweet & Indulgent

Sweet & Indulgent

Kefir Ice Cream with Blackcurrant Preserve

Morozchenoye s chernoy smorodinoy varenye

Tangy kefir puts this dessert somewhere between a frozen yoghurt and a creamy ice cream. The custard I use as its base is inspired by the *Van Leeuwen Artisan Ice Cream* book, in which the most interesting flavours are paired – it encouraged me to experiment and create an ice cream using kefir, a staple in our home. You'll need an ice-cream maker for this recipe; be sure to check the instructions before use, as you may need to pop the bowl in the freezer before using. My dad loves to top this with blackcurrant varenye (an Eastern-European whole-fruit preserve), but you could use any of the preserves on pages 84–89.

MAKES 1 x 1L (34FL OZ) TUB OF ICE CREAM AND 1 x 550ML (19FL OZ) JAR OF BLACKCURRANT PRESERVE

For the kefir ice cream
375ml (13fl oz) double (heavy) cream
2 Tbsp milk
130g (4½oz) caster (superfine) sugar
pinch of salt
8 large egg yolks
375ml (13fl oz) kefir

For the blackcurrant varenye
500g (1lb 2oz) blackcurrants
  (frozen or fresh)
250g (9oz) sugar

First make the ice cream. Set a heatproof bowl over a medium-sized saucepan, one-third filled with water, and place over a medium heat. Add the cream and milk to the heatproof bowl. Bring the water to a simmer and stir the cream and milk together. When the mixture is warm, add the sugar and salt, stirring until dissolved and the mixture is hot but not boiling. There will be a bit of steam from the simmering water so adjust the heat to make sure it's not too intense.

In a separate medium bowl, whisk the egg yolks. Continue to whisk and add 1 tablespoon of the hot cream into the yolks, then another 2 tablespoons, then a more generous splash. Continually whisking, add the rest of the hot cream.

Immediately transfer the mixture to the original heatproof bowl over the pan. Increase the heat to medium–high and whisk the mixture continuously to thicken it, adjusting the heat if needed. You should feel the custard start to thicken and see steam rising from the pan. Keep whisking gently for about 10–15 minutes. When it looks and feels thicker, dip a wooden spoon into the custard, then run your finger across the back of the spoon. If you can form a line through the custard, it's ready, but if the line closes up again continue to cook and test again. Meanwhile, set up an ice bath – fill up a bowl with water and some ice. Set aside.

When the custard is ready, use a cloth to take the bowl off the pan. Give the kefir a good shake in the bottle before pouring it into the bowl and whisking it through well. Place the bowl over an ice bath. Stir it occasionally while it cools – about 10–15 minutes. Cover the surface with cling film (plastic wrap) and place in the refrigerator overnight or for at least 8 hours. As it cools, it will thicken further. When ready, transfer the custard to your ice cream maker. Following the instructions on your machine, churn for approximately 1 hour or until thickened. For soft-serve style, serve immediately, or transfer into containers and place in the freezer for 2 hours before serving. The ice cream will last up to 3 months in the freezer.

To make the blackcurrant varenye, place the blackcurrants, sugar and 2 tablespoons of water in a bowl and stir so that the sugar coats the fruit. Leave for 15 minutes, then transfer to a saucepan and bring to a simmer, stirring occasionally. Once the mixture starts to bubble and simmer, cook it at a low simmer for 15–20 minutes, stirring occasionally. Transfer to a sterilized jar and seal tightly with a lid. Cool and store in the refrigerator until ready to serve with the ice cream. The preserve will last for 2–3 months unopened in the refrigerator.

Apple and Cinnamon Sponge Cake

Yablochnaya Sharlotka

During visits to Eastern Europe, we would often go on road trips driving between countries. On those long drives we would always pack for a roadside picnic. For something sweet, my mum would make this apple sponge cake: it's easy to travel with and even easier to make.

SERVES 6

butter, for greasing
4 eggs
210g (7½oz) caster (superfine) sugar
150g (5¼oz) plain (all-purpose) flour, sifted
⅓ tsp bicarbonate of soda (baking soda)
1 tsp apple cider vinegar
small pinch of salt
3 apples, washed
50g (1¾oz) walnuts, chopped (optional)
1 Tbsp ground cinnamon
1 tsp icing (confectioner's) sugar (optional)

Preheat the oven to 180°C fan/200°C/400°F/Gas mark 6. Butter and line a 22cm (8in) springform cake tin with baking paper. In an electric stand mixer fitted with the whisk attachment (or using an electric hand whisk), beat the eggs and sugar on medium–high speed for about 10 minutes until the mixture is light and airy and has doubled in volume.

Reduce the speed and add the flour slowly to combine. In a small cup, mix the bicarbonate of soda with the vinegar until fizzing, then add to the cake batter with the pinch of salt. Continue to whisk for another 30 seconds.

Halve and core the apples and slice into thin wedge shapes. Roughly chop the walnuts.

Once the cake batter is thick and fluffy, pour half of it into the lined cake tin. Add about two-thirds of the sliced apples over the surface, so that they are fairly evenly spread. Sprinkle the apples with a layer of the cinnamon. Pour the rest of the batter over the top and cover with the walnuts (some will sink into the cake during cooking). Arrange the remaining apple slices over the surface, slightly overlapping, pressing them lightly into the batter. Place on the lower shelf of the oven and bake for 1 hour until slightly risen and a skewer inserted into the middle comes out clean.

Remove the cake from the oven and allow to cool slightly. After 15 minutes remove the cake from the tin, leave to cool and dust with icing sugar, if you wish.

Sweet & Indulgent

Sweet & Indulgent

Monika's Plum Rogaliki

Rahaliki sa slivovym varenniem

My babushka Lida's lifelong best friend, Monika, was always up for a dinner party whenever we visited. Walking into her apartment in Baranavichy, a table would be set and covered with so many plates and platters of food that you could barely see the tablecloth, including a crystal cake stand that she'd fill with these freshly baked plum rogaliki. During one of my last trips, I spent an afternoon making these with her. She showed me how to roll, fill and bake them as we sipped first on coffee and then *nalivka* (homemade fruit wine) while the buttery pastries in the oven filled her home with their incredible smell.

These flaky biscuits have depth, texture and softness all at once. There are versions of rogaliki made throughout Poland, Ukraine, Belarus, Lithuania and beyond. I like to make my own plum jam for these (see page 86). I have also made these with apricot jam, lingonberry jam, and a crushed walnut, cinnamon and sugar filling.

MAKES 32 ROGALIKI

125ml (4fl oz) lukewarm milk
2 Tbsp sugar
4g (⅛oz) fast-action dried yeast
350g (12oz) plain (all-purpose) flour,
    plus extra for dusting
small pinch of salt
200g (7oz) butter, diced and at
    room temperature, plus extra
    for greasing
270g (9½oz) plum jam (jelly)
egg wash (1 small egg beaten with
    a dash of milk)
icing (confectioner's) sugar, for dusting

Put the lukewarm milk in a bowl and mix in the sugar and yeast. Set aside for 10 minutes or until frothy.

Sift the flour into the bowl of an electric stand mixer fitted with a dough hook. Add the salt and butter, then pour the yeast mixture into the bowl. Mix for 5 minutes on a slow–medium speed. (You can also make the dough by hand: mix the ingredients together in a bowl and then knead by hand until smooth.) Once the dough has come together, shape it into a smooth round ball and place in a buttered bowl, covered with cling film (plastic wrap). Leave to rest and rise slightly for about 1½ hours. It's quite a heavy dough, so don't expect it to rise as much as lighter yeast doughs. It should look dense but slightly expanded.

Preheat the oven to 180°C fan/200°C/400°F/Gas mark 6. Line two baking trays with baking paper. Remove the dough from the bowl and place on a lightly floured surface. Use your hands to shape it into an even cylinder, then score with a

Sweet & Indulgent

sharp knife to mark where to slice it into four equal pieces. Slice through the score marks and shape your four pieces into balls.

Lightly flour your worktop. Place one piece of dough in the centre and use a lightly floured rolling pin to roll it into a roughly even circle that is 2mm (⅟₁₆in) thin. Cut the circle into eight even triangles by first cutting it in half, then into quarters and then eighths. Place a teaspoon of jam 1cm (½in) from the curved edge of the first triangle. Lift the edge and fold it over the jam, then roll it until you reach the point. Curve in the two ends to form a crescent shape. Repeat with the remaining seven triangles. Transfer the rogaliki to the baking trays as you make them – they're fine to sit side by side in the tray.

Repeat with the remaining dough pieces, rolling, cutting and filling to make eight rogaliki from each piece and, once your trays are full, brush the tops with the egg wash. Bake for 25–30 minutes or until risen and slightly golden in colour (the timing depends on your particular oven so check them regularly). Remove from the oven and place on wire racks. When the rogaliki have completely cooled, sift icing sugar over the top. These are best eaten fresh on the day, but they will last up to a week if stored in an airtight container, and can easily be frozen.

Sour Cherry Kefir Pie
Pirog z visniaj

My family have always loved a pastry with a bit of texture, so I make a dough that is somewhere in between fluffy and flaky, enriched with kefir, with a lovely sour cherry filling. The pastry can be kept overnight in the fridge.

SERVES 8

For the filling
1kg (2lb 4oz) pitted sour cherries
   (fresh or frozen)
210g (7½oz) caster (superfine) sugar
2 Tbsp cornflour (cornstarch), mixed
   with 2 Tbsp cold water

For the pastry
450g (1lb) plain (all-purpose) flour, sifted,
   plus extra for dusting
60g (2¼oz) caster (superfine) sugar
pinch of salt
300g (10½oz) cold unsalted butter,
   plus extra for greasing
½ tsp bicarbonate of soda (baking soda)
1 tsp white vinegar
1 Tbsp kefir
1 Tbsp water
egg wash (1 small egg beaten
   with a dash of milk)
soured cream, double (heavy) cream
   or crème fraîche, to serve

Put the sour cherries and sugar in a large saucepan. Bring to the boil while stirring to dissolve the sugar, then reduce to a gentle simmer over a medium heat. After 5 minutes, increase the heat, add the cornflour slurry and cook, stirring, for another 5 minutes. Set aside to cool, stirring occasionally.

Mix the flour, sugar and salt in a large bowl. Coarsely grate the butter over the top. Work the mixture with your fingers until it resembles breadcrumbs. In a small bowl mix the bicarbonate of soda with the vinegar until fizzing, then add the kefir and water and add to the flour bowl. Roughly combine using a fork, then use your hands to gently knead the dough for about 5 minutes, before shaping into a ball. Divide the dough in two pieces, with one slightly larger. Shape into discs and cover with cling film (plastic wrap). Refrigerate for at least 2 hours. If using the next day, remove the dough 1 hour before rolling out.

When you're ready to cook, preheat the oven to 180°C fan/200°C/400°F/Gas mark 6. Grease a 22cm (8½in) pie dish. Roll out the larger piece of dough on a lightly floured surface so that it's large enough to form the base and sides of your pie. Transfer it to the buttered dish. Use your fingers to gently press it into the base and prick with a fork in several places. Add the filling to the pie.

Roll out the second piece of dough large enough to cover the top of the pie. Place on top of the filling. Seal the edges by pinching and squeezing them together tightly. Cut a hole in the centre of the pie, then brush the top with the egg wash.

Bake in the oven for 50 minutes or until golden brown. Cover with foil if the pastry is darkening too fast. Let stand for 30 minutes before serving. Serve with your choice of cream.

Sweet & Indulgent

Sweet & Indulgent

Chocolate and Hazelnut Babka with Cognac Glaze

Shokoladna babka

This babka is a perfect example of how practice makes perfect. The recipe makes two wreaths: so make one for yourself and gift one to a friend or neighbour, especially during a festive season. My babushkas rarely baked in small batches, particularly yeasted doughs, the thinking being that if you're turning on the oven and using energy, you may as well bake a generous amount.

MAKES 2 WREATHS

250ml (9fl oz) lukewarm milk
14g (½oz) fast-action dried yeast
4 Tbsp sugar
800g (1lb 12oz) plain (all-purpose) flour, plus extra for dusting
250g (9oz) butter, diced, plus extra for greasing
3 eggs
150ml (5fl oz) soured cream
pinch of salt

For the filling
150g (5½oz) chocolate (70% cocoa), roughly chopped
100g (3½oz) butter
200g (7oz) brown sugar
30g (1oz) cacao
1 tsp ground cinnamon
pinch of salt
30g (1oz) hazelnuts, roughly chopped

For the glaze
50g (1¾oz) brown sugar
2 Tbsp cognac
4 Tbsp water

Put the lukewarm milk in a bowl and mix in the yeast, 1 tablespoon of the sugar and 1 tablespoon of the flour. Whisk quickly and set aside for 10 minutes until frothy. Put the butter in a pan and melt over a medium heat, then set aside to cool slightly. Whisk the eggs in a medium bowl and then slowly pour the cooled butter into the eggs, while whisking, followed by the soured cream, and whisk again until smooth.

Sift the remaining flour into the bowl of a stand mixer fitted with a dough hook and then add the salt and the rest of the sugar for the dough. Pour in the egg and cream mixture, along with the activated yeast mixture. Mix on low–medium speed for 5 minutes or until well combined.

Remove and form into a round shape, using extra flour if needed but keep in mind this is a moist dough owing to the soured cream. Place in a lightly greased bowl, cover with a towel and set aside to rise and double in size. If your kitchen is cold, you can put the dough in a heatproof bowl and place in a conventional oven set at 40°C (104°F) – allow up to 1 hour.

Just before rolling out the dough, make the filling. Set a small heatproof bowl on top of a saucepan one-third filled with water and place over a gentle heat. When the water is simmering, put the chocolate, butter, sugar, cacao, cinnamon and salt in the bowl and stir. Once melted, set aside.

Preheat the oven to 180°C fan/200°C/400°F/Gas mark 6 and line a baking tray with baking paper. Once the dough

Sweet & Indulgent

has doubled in size, transfer it to a lightly floured surface and divide into two equal parts about 840g (1lb 14oz) each. Flour the worktop generously and roll out the first piece to a rectangle roughly 55 x 25cm (22 x 10in); it doesn't have to be exact. Use a spatula to spread half the chocolate filling evenly over the surface, then sprinkle with half the hazelnuts. Leave the second piece covered.

Use your hands to roll up the dough, starting with one long side and rolling to form one very long roll, ensuring an even width of around 8cm (3¼in). Leaving one short end intact, partially divide the roll into three long pieces, ready to braid. Turn each piece so that the chocolate filling is facing upwards. Braid the three pieces into a plait, then attach the ends by pressing them together tightly. Place the wreath on the lined baking tray. Let it rise even more before baking, if needed; though, most of the time it's good to go straight into the oven. Bake for 50–60 minutes.

Meanwhile, make the second wreath and bake it on the bottom shelf at the same time as the first (or leave to rise further in your kitchen until the first one is baked).

Once both wreaths are baked, make the glaze by putting the sugar, cognac and water into a small saucepan and simmering for 1 minute. While they are still warm, brush the top of the wreaths with this glaze.

Slice and enjoy fresh or store in an airtight container to eat over the week ahead.

Sweet & Indulgent

Sweet & Indulgent

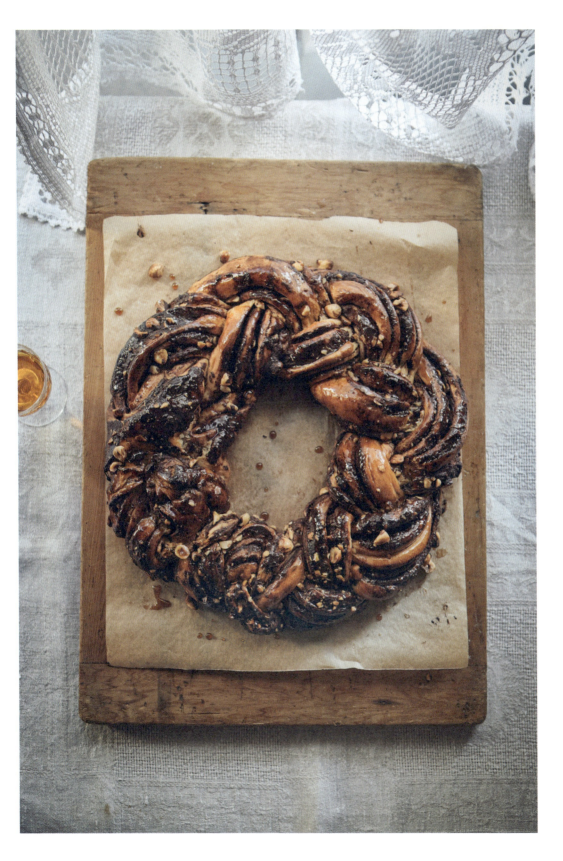

Sweet & Indulgent

Plum, Apple and Sour Cherry Rye Crumble

Fruktovyy pyrih

In autumn, when evenings get cooler I always want to turn on the oven and get baking. I use the last of the end of summer plums, the first of the local apples and the sour cherries I have saved in my freezer – some of my favourite Eastern European ingredients that make a sweet and sour combination. The addition of rye flour and walnuts adds texture and thickness to the crumble so there'll be a nice bite to it.

SERVES 6-8

For the base

5 medium–large plums, pitted and
    sliced into wedges
5 apples, cored and sliced into wedges
150g (5¼oz) brown sugar
250g (9oz) pitted sour cherries
    (frozen or fresh)

For the crumble

130g (4½oz) rye flour
150g (5¼oz) plain (all-purpose) flour
1 tsp ground cinnamon
pinch of salt
200g (7oz) brown sugar
80g (3oz) oats
½ tsp baking powder
60g (2¼oz) walnuts, roughly chopped
180g (6¼oz) butter, melted, plus extra
    for greasing
soured cream or crème fraîche, to serve

Preheat the oven to 180°C fan/200°C/400°F/Gas mark 6. Grease a 33 x 20 x 5cm (13 x 8 x 2in) deep-sided baking dish. Put the plums, apples and sugar into a large saucepan over a medium–high heat and stir while the sugar coating the fruit dissolves. Keep simmering for 10 minutes so that the fruit slightly reduces and softens. Stir in the sour cherries, and cook for a further 5 minutes. Transfer to the baking dish and spread out in an even layer.

To make the crumble, put the flours, cinnamon, salt, sugar, oats, baking powder and walnuts in a large mixing bowl. Mix everything together. Pour the melted butter into the bowl and use a fork to give it a good mix. Use your hands to transfer the crumble over the fruit in the dish. Spread it evenly without pressing it down.

Bake for about 30 minutes or until the top is slightly golden and the sauce from the fruit is sticky and bubbling at the edges of the crumble. (You may want to add a large tray underneath if it starts to overflow a bit.) Remove from the oven and serve in large spoonfuls with cream on top.

Tip: Another trio I love is apples, pears and blackcurrants (frozen blackcurrants are fine). Use 5 apples, 4 pears and 220g (7¾oz) blackcurrants and follow the method above.

Sweet & Indulgent

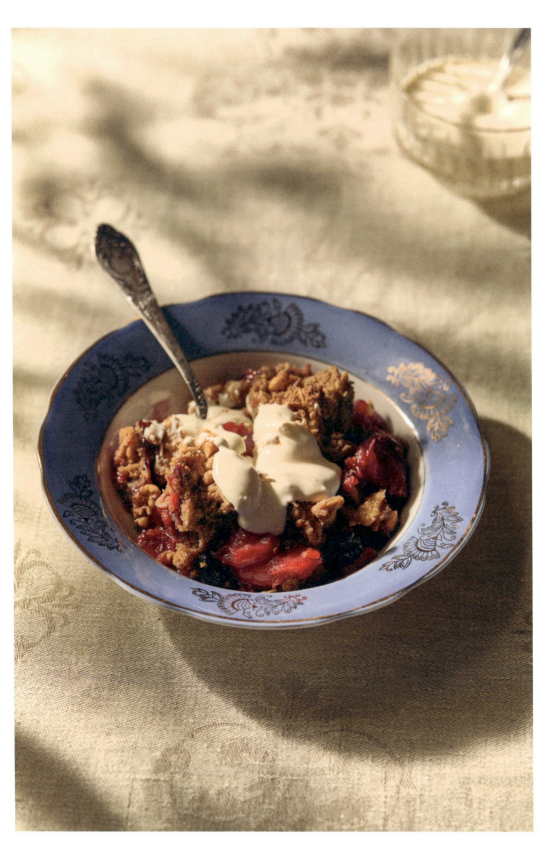

Chocolate Buckwheat Cake with Sour Cherry Sauce
Šakaladny tort

I've made this cake many times for occasions when I wanted to make something simple, delicious and beautiful. It's lovely and earthy – use a thick, luscious soured cream, or give it a quick whisk to thicken before use. Using buckwheat flour also means this recipe is a good gluten-free option.

SERVES 6–8

200g (7oz) butter, diced small
200g (7oz) dark chocolate (70% cocoa), chopped into small chunks
2 Tbsp espresso
1 tsp vanilla extract
¼ tsp salt
250g (9oz) brown sugar
5 eggs
100g (3½oz) buckwheat flour
325ml (11fl oz) soured cream
100g (3½oz) walnuts, finely chopped or blitzed in a food processor

For the sauce
100g (3½oz) pitted sour cherries (frozen or fresh)
100g (3½oz) sugar
1 Tbsp cornflour (cornstarch), mixed with 1 Tbsp cold water

Preheat the oven to 180°C fan/200°C/400°F/Gas mark 6. Line the base and sides of a 23cm (9in) springform cake tin with baking paper. Set a medium heatproof bowl over a small saucepan of simmering water. Put the butter, chocolate, espresso, vanilla and salt in the heatproof bowl and stir occasionally. Once everything has melted, mix thoroughly, then remove the bowl from the pan and set aside.

Put the sugar and eggs in the bowl of a stand mixer and whisk on a medium–high speed for about 7 minutes or until the mixture has increased in size and is light and frothy (or use an electric hand whisk). Sift the buckwheat flour into the bowl with the melted chocolate mixture. Use a hand whisk to mix the flour through completely. Mix in 125ml (4fl oz) of the soured cream.

Once the sugar and egg mixture is light and frothy, pour the chocolate mixture into the bowl. Use a spatula to fold in until well combined – this might take a good couple of minutes. Try not to overfold, though, so that the mixture remains airy. Add the walnuts and fold through a few more times.

Pour the batter into the cake tin and place in the oven to cook for 30–40 minutes or until the top has risen slightly and it looks firm in the centre. Remove the cake from the oven and let it cool for a few minutes before turning onto a wire rack.

Mix the ingredients for the sauce in a saucepan and bring to a simmer. Cook gently for 10 minutes, stirring often. Leave to cool.

Give the rest of the soured cream a stir, then spoon over the surface of the cooled cake. Top with the sour cherry sauce.

Honey, Walnut and Soured Cream Cake

Kutuzovsky tort

Looking back through the recipes from my dad's Ukrainian babushka, this one in particular stood out. Zinaida was a celebrated cook and cake-maker. Now when I look at her recipes I can see she would create magic with just a few basic ingredients, a reflection of the times and the way many people cooked.

Traditionally, Mum and Zina would use their hands to flatten the pastry layers – the result was a thickish pastry, so if you'd like to try that method do have a go. For ease and thinner layers, we often also roll it out now. It's best made the day before serving, so that the cake layers soften and are easy to slice.

Sweet & Indulgent

SERVES 8-10

For the pastry

240g (8½oz) unsalted butter,
  at room temperature
200g (7oz) brown sugar
4 Tbsp good-quality runny honey
2 eggs at room temperature
1 tsp bicarbonate of soda (baking soda)
2 tsp apple cider vinegar
600g (1lb 5oz) plain (all-purpose) flour,
  sifted, plus extra for dusting

For the cream

200g (7oz) unsalted butter, cubed
  and softened
210g (7½oz) caster (superfine) sugar
600ml (21fl oz) soured cream,
  at room temperature
6 Tbsp lemon juice (more or less,
  to taste)
150g (5½oz) walnuts, very
  finely chopped

To make the pastry, put the butter and sugar in the bowl of a stand mixer with a whisk attachment, or add to a bowl and use an electric hand whisk. Whisk on medium–high speed until well combined. Add the honey and eggs and whisk to combine. Mix the bicarbonate of soda and vinegar in a small cup until fizzing, then pour this into the bowl and mix again. Use a spatula to scrape down the sides. Add the flour and whisk on a medium speed for a few minutes until everything comes together to form a sticky dough. It should be quite heavy; add a little more flour if it's a humid day.

Remove the dough from the bowl and use your hands to shape it into a log on a lightly floured surface. Divide into seven roughly equal pieces.

Preheat the oven to 180°C fan/200°C/400°F/Gas mark 6. Select a medium-sized round plate: this is your template for the pastry layers. Prepare seven pieces of baking paper, 2–3cm (1in) wider than the plate. Coat the rolling pin in a little flour and roll out each piece of dough directly on the baking paper into very thin rounds (about 2mm/¹⁄₁₆in thick). Place the plate gently over the rolled-out dough sheets, one at a time, and use a knife to cut around the plate. Use a fork to prick over the surface of each layer. Reserve the offcuts from each layer, combine them and roll out into a small disc of the same thickness to use for making the crumbs later.

Transfer each piece of dough, still on its baking sheet, to a baking tray. Cook each layer, one at a time, for about 8–10 minutes or until lightly golden – if using a fan oven, you can cook the layers in batches to speed things up. Once ready, remove the pastry, with baking paper, from the hot tray and set aside to cool. I use a few trays interchangeably.

Sweet & Indulgent

Once you have baked all the layers, place the disc made from the offcuts on some baking paper on a tray and cook for 8–10 minutes. Cool and then crush in a bowl to resemble toasted breadcrumbs. Set aside.

To make the cream, make sure you remove the soured cream from the refrigerator at least 45 minutes before using. Put the butter and sugar into the bowl of a stand mixer (or mix using an electric hand whisk). Whisk on low–medium speed until well combined and then add the soured cream and lemon juice, keeping the speed quite low so that the whisking doesn't stiffen the cream. Continue to whisk for 1 minute and then remove and finish by hand, whisking until the cream is soft, creamy and the sugar has dissolved. If it's too thick, adjust by adding more lemon juice or water.

To assemble the cake, place the first pastry layer on a cake stand or large flat plate that you'll be serving the cake on. Spread a few heaped tablespoons of the cream over the entire surface. Sprinkle the cream with some of the finely chopped walnuts, then repeat the layering with the remaining pastry, cream and walnuts. Sprinkle the crushed pastry crumbs on top.

Keep in the refrigerator overnight, and take it out around 15 minutes before serving.

Tip: Experiment with flavours, like adding chopped pitted prunes to the cream. I also like to add a thin layer of homemade strawberry jam or blackcurrant varenye (see page 178).

Napoleon Layer Cake
Napoleon

My great-babushka Zinaida made this cake for my first birthday. She carefully baked each layer at her home and then Mum travelled with the layers for the cake safely packaged in an overnight train from Kharkiv in Ukraine, to Baranavichy in Belarus. She made it in advance so that all Mum needed to do was the cream and assembling. Many years later, we had this cake at our wedding celebration in Sydney. Similar to *mille-feuille*, but rather than being thick crunchy pastry layers, the layers are delicately soft and melt and have a tiny bit of crispiness on the edges.

MAKES 20 SMALL SQUARES (ENOUGH FOR 10 PEOPLE WHO ALL WANT SECONDS!)

For the pastry
450g (16oz) plain (all-purpose) flour, sifted, plus extra for dusting
300g (10½oz) cold unsalted butter (kept as a block)
1 egg
pinch of fine salt
180ml (6fl oz) cold water
1 Tbsp white vinegar

For the cream
1 litre (35fl oz) milk
260g (9¼oz) caster (superfine) sugar
4 egg yolks
2 Tbsp plain (all-purpose) flour, sifted
300g (10½oz) unsalted butter, very soft and chopped into small pieces
⅓ tsp vanilla bean paste

For the pastry, put the flour in a large bowl and coat the cold butter block with flour so that you can grip it easily. Coarsely grate the butter directly into the bowl. Work the butter and flour mixture through your fingers until it resembles breadcrumbs. In a separate bowl mix together the egg, salt, water and vinegar. Pour this into the centre of the flour mixture and mix with a fork to bring it together, then knead for 5 minutes in the bowl.

Transfer the dough to a lightly floured surface, flour your hands and knead until smooth, adding a bit of extra flour if the dough feels too moist. Shape into a round disc and cover tightly in cling film (plastic wrap). Place in the refrigerator for 2 hours.

Meanwhile, pour the milk into a large saucepan and gently heat until hot but not boiling. In a bowl, mix the sugar and egg yolks together. Add 6 tablespoons of the warm milk and the 2 tablespoons of flour and whisk until smooth and thick.

Once the milk is hot, slowly add the egg mixture, a little at a time, whisking to combine. Increase the heat to medium–high and cook for 5–7 minutes until the mixture starts to thicken to make a custard, continuously whisking so the custard doesn't burn or stick to the base. Once the custard has thickened, remove it from the heat and pour into a large bowl. Set aside to cool completely and cover the custard with cling film – this prevents a skin forming.

Sweet & Indulgent

Once the dough has rested for 2 hours, remove from the refrigerator and divide into nine pieces, each weighing about 100g (3½oz), plus an extra piece that should weigh about 70g (2½oz). Wrap each in cling film and put back in the refrigerator.

Preheat the oven to 180°C fan/200°C/400°F/Gas mark 6. Line two baking trays with baking paper. Take one of the 100g (3½oz) pastry pieces, shape it into a square and place on a lightly floured surface. Begin to roll it into a large rectangle, roughly 40 x 28cm (16 x 11¼in). The pastry should be very thin, almost like filo (phyllo). Dust with more flour if needed, and rotate and flip the pastry as you roll. Don't worry about perfection here.

Transfer the first rectangle to the lined tray and place in the oven. Cook for 6–8 minutes until the pastry is puffed up and golden. Meanwhile roll out the next piece of dough to the same size, transfer to the second tray and place in the oven for 6–8 minutes as you take out the first. Transfer the first cooked layer to a wire rack to cool. Continue to roll out and cook nine rectangles, swapping the trays as they cook, and cooling them in sequence.

Recipe continues overleaf.

Finally, roll out the small piece of dough as thinly as possible and cook on a lined tray for about 6 minutes. Remove from the oven, let it cool and crumble into a small bowl. Set aside.

Now you can finish the cream filling. The butter for the filling needs to be very soft so that it's easy to mix. Mash the butter in a bowl until pliable, then add 3 tablespoons of the cooled custard and use a fork or small sturdy whisk to mix it through. Gradually add the custard in increasing amounts, combining each time, being careful not to overwhisk – see tip, below. When all the custard is added, add the vanilla and whisk to combine until smooth. If your cream seems a little on the runny side, don't worry as it will become slightly firmer while the assembled cake sits in the refrigerator.

To assemble the cake, select a baking tray that will accommodate the pastry layers (and fit in your refrigerator). Place one of the pastry layers on top. Add about 10 tablespoons of cream to the pastry layer and lightly spread it over the surface with the back of a spoon, gently crushing any air bubbles in the pastry. Repeat the layering of pastry and cream. Once you have added the cream to the last layer, sprinkle over the crumbled pastry. Your cake may seem quite tall but it will drop slightly as the pastry soaks overnight.

Place in the refrigerator, uncovered, for at least 8 hours or overnight. Remove from the refrigerator 15 minutes before serving so that the cream softens slightly. Slice into small squares and serve.

This keeps for a few days, though the cream continues to soak through the pastry layers.

Tip: When making the cream filling, if the mixture splits don't panic! Set a heatproof bowl over a small or medium pan of simmering water. Transfer the custard to the heatproof bowl and whisk for 30 seconds or however long it needs to restore its creamy texture, adjusting the heat as needed. Transfer the bowl to the fridge for a few minutes to ensure the filling is cool before assembling the layers.

Stockists

GENERAL

Australia:
Deli Hub
Stores in St Ives and Maroubra, NSW.
Find them on Facebook.

Magda's Euro Delicatessen
Roseville, NSW.
Find them on Facebook.

Simon Johnson
Retail stores in NSW, Victoria, WA.
Online provider of imported and
home-grown quality food.
simonjohnson.com

Stolichniy Minimart
Eastlakes, NSW.
Find them on Facebook.

UK:
Dacha Shop
London, England
dachashop.co.uk

USA:
Babushka – Grandma's Deli
Hollywood, California
Find them on Facebook or email
babushka.deli@yahoo.com

Emish Market
Fife, Washington
emishmarket.com

Netcost Markets (retail stores)
New York
netcostmarket.com

Roman Russian Market
Portland, Oregon
romanrussianmarket.com

MEAT, POULTRY & FISH

Australia:
Feather and Bone
Stores in Sydney and Waverley, NSW
(also home delivery).
featherandbone.com.au

Alaska Crab
Matraville, NSW
alaskancrabco.com.au

Willoughby Seafoods
Sydney, NSW
Find them on Facebook.

DAIRY

Australia:
Burraduc Buffalo Farm
Bungwahl, NSW
burraducbuffalo.com.au

Cheese Lavka
Sydney, NSW
Find them on Facebook or email:
tvoroglavka@gmail.com

BREAD/FLOURS

Australia:
Baker Bleu
Stores in Victoria and NSW
bakerbleu.com.au

Flour Shop
Sydney, NSW
flourshop.com.au

Wholegrain Milling Co
Gunnedah, NSW
wholegrain.com.au

UK:
Karaway Bakery
London, England
karawaybakery.com

Shipton Mill
Tetbury, Gloucestershire, England
Organic, stone-ground flours.
Available online for UK and Ireland.
shipton-mill.com

USA:
Bob's Red Mill
Milwaukie, Oregon
Wholegrain store/bakery.
Also available online.
bobsredmill.com

Janie's Mill
Ashkun, Illinois
Organic, stone-ground flours.
Available online.
janiesmill.com

Tartine Bakery
Locations in California;
also available online (ship nationally).
tartinebakery.com

PANTRY

Australia:
Broth Bar & Larder
Bronte, NSW
Organic wholefood free from
artificial or processed ingredients.
Available online (ship nationally).
staraniseorganic.com/broth-bar-larder

The Essential Ingredient
Stores in NSW and Victoria
essentialingredient.com.au

The Fermentary
Vegetables, drinks and cultures.
thefermentary.com.au

Tamada
Sydney, NSW
Premium products from Georgia
including wines, sunflower oil
and adjika.
tamada.com.au

UK:
Clearspring
London, England
Oils, pastes, grains, pulses,
dried mushrooms and other
store-cupboard essentials.
clearspring.co.uk

FRESH/MARKETS

Australia:
Carriageworks Farmers Markets
Sydney, NSW
www.carriageworks.com.au

Galluzzo Fruiterers
Sydney, NSW
Find on Facebook, Instagram or
email galluzzofruiterers@gmail.com

Kurrawong Organics
kurrawongorganics.com.au

Prahran Market
Melbourne, Victoria
prahranmarket.com.au

FROZEN

Australia:
Forestway Fresh
Terrey Hills, NSW
forestwayfresh.com

Index

About the Author

My career in food began in my late twenties, when I appeared on *Masterchef Australia*. I started to experiment with flavours and techniques far removed from the home-cooked food I grew up with. Stints doing work experience in Sydney restaurants widened my repertoire and honed my skills, and I spent a period cooking, writing and photographing for brands. But as time went on, I felt something calling me home. The realization eventually came in 2017, during a visit to Ukraine and Belarus with my mum.

We arrived in Kyiv in summer and it hit me: I had forgotten the food of my heritage. There it was, in all its colours, scents, flavours and beauty; on market stalls, on the kitchen tables, in the villages, cities, forests. I saw it with fresh eyes. It was time to discover, or rediscover, the familiar food of my family and somehow, one day, to share it. I started asking questions: what was so special about these recipes, ingredients and traditions that I had followed most my life? On countless occasions I sat with loved ones, listening to, documenting and recording their stories.

These days, I am a recipe developer, food writer and food stylist based in Sydney. I am passionate about connecting food with community, and I host workshops where I teach home cooks how to make pyrizhky, honey cake, cabbage rolls and other signature Eastern European dishes. My hope with my first cookbook is to inspire you to make the heart-felt, soul-filled recipes that have been passed down the generations of my family.

Acknowledgements

This book started in my heart and mind many years ago. Looking back, the best part of this project was the journey of discovery and of meeting so many incredible people. Bringing these recipes to life has connected me to some of the most wonderful humans.

Thank you to my mum, Elena, your love of home cooking is the reason that I had to write this book. You supported me from the start, taught me how to cook and passed on your love of tradition. I will treasure your dedication to this book and the adventures that we have had along the way. I couldn't have done it without you. Thank you to my dad for teaching me to never give up and get things done.

Babushka Lida, wherever you are now, you have given me so much – your recipes and even your tablecloths have shaped the pages of this book. I miss you and wish you could be here to see it come to life.

Babushka Liana, I am so grateful for all the knowledge you continue to share with me. I wish we could go back in time to your dacha in Kharkiv. Thank you for everything.

A huge thanks also to my brother, Anthony, for your help and appetite on the shoot, and Beau Janney, for your endless support. Thank you both for your feedback along the way.

Jane Novak, my incredible agent, I nearly put writing a cookbook to rest, but something called me to you. You valued these recipes and stories so much and made this book land in the best of hands.

Stacey Cleworth, thank you from the bottom of my heart for making it all happen. You made the biggest dream of my life come true. Thank you to Sarah Lavelle for also believing in this book. Ellie Spence, it has been a breeze working with you, thank you for your patience on all the edits. To Stephanie Evans, you made it all flow with your thoughtful approach and attention to detail. I learnt so much from you. Thank you to Sarah Epton for proofreading so diligently!

Gemma Hayden, your beautiful design quite literally made this all come to life. Thank you for your dedication and the thoughtful touch you added. Katherine Case, you captured the vision and set a stunning tone for the book. Thank you for all the work you did behind the scenes for the front cover and more. Meredith Walker, as soon as I saw your art, I knew it would be a perfect fit for the book, so thank you for creating a front cover that encapsulates it all.

Karen Fisher, every step of the way you truly believed in this book. You have so pivotal in its creation. Thank you for the most beautiful photos, as well as your patience, persistence, insight and support. I am eternally grateful to have gone on this journey with you.

Breda, it was a dream having you in the kitchen, with the pots bubbling, the ovens cranked on high and the the the smell of freshly cooked pies in the air. You were always 10 steps ahead. Let's cook together again soon!

Jessica Hanson, your natural eye for styling made all the pieces come together. Thank you for your thoughtful touches and the late-night sourcing chats.

Tess Thyregod, thank you for stepping in with so much talent and dedication. Amy Bramble, thank you for everything, especially for braving the rain to get the perfect shot!

Thank you to my dear relatives and family friends: my auntie Marina, uncle Sasha, my cousins, Anna and Vlad Volkov – I'll always treasure the time you took to teach me about our family recipes. I love and miss you all. Marisha Pekarchyk, for teaching me so much about baking and being part of the journey from the beginning. Forever grateful to Vladimir Borovik, Slava and Lusien Bankevich, Monica and Olga Salash, Luda and Leonid Teniakovy, Luba and Sergei Kuntsevich, Nina Samuseva, Julia Konovalov and Alexey Karol. I can't wait to cook with you again one day. Lena Keis, your family heirloom pieces were a beautiful addition to the pages.

A huge thanks to Kristy Woodruff, Katrina Thomasson and Tana Stojanov for being such supportive friends. Katrina you tested the recipes so diligently. Thank you to Olia Koutseridi for your recipe testing and knowledgeable advice. Georgie and Joe Dolling, I'll always be grateful for our first phone conversation that helped to spark my cookbook endeavour.

Alissa Timoshkina, I am grateful for our chats, your support and mentoring – you have always inspired me. Olia Hercules, when I visited Ukraine and met you it was a life-changing trip; you are a huge inspiration to me. Tessa Kiros, thank you for your generosity and support, from the other side of the world, all those years ago. Lucy Leonardi, thank you for connecting me with Jane. Paola Bacchia, I am grateful for your words of encouragement. Vikki and Helena, I don't think we'd be here if you didn't push me to try again, thank you for everything. Daen Lia and Maya Mesimeris, your support was always felt. Laurie Green and Larissa Takchi, for providing the beautiful produce for the shoot.

To my husband Antonio, thank you for being on this journey with me and always believing in me – I love you. And to our two new additions to our family, Isabella and Samuel, who were both born during the different stages of creating this book, I hope you'll cook these recipes one day.

To you, the reader, for picking up this book. I hope you enjoy it and that it finds a new home on your bookshelf – thank you from the bottom of my heart.

Quadrille, Penguin Random House UK, One Embassy Gardens,
8 Viaduct Gardens, London SW11 7BW

Quadrille Publishing Limited is part of the Penguin Random House
group of companies whose addresses can be found at global.
penguinrandomhouse.com

Penguin
Random House
UK

Text © Anastasia Zolotarev 2025
Photography © Karen Fisher 2025, except pages 5, 13, 35 (left),
    36 (left), 45, 61, 63, 75, 80, 83, 86, 122 (left), 174 (left), 203
    © Anastasia Zolotarev 2025
Cover Illustration © Meredith Walker 2025
Design © Quadrille 2025

Published by Quadrille in 2025

www.penguin.co.uk
A CIP catalogue record for this book is available from the British Library

ISBN 978 1 83783 183 8
10 9 8 7 6 5 4 3 2 1

Managing Director Sarah Lavelle
Senior Commissioning Editor Stacey Cleworth
Editorial Assistant Ellie Spence
Senior Designer Gemma Hayden
Cover Design and Illustration Meredith Walker
Photography Karen Fisher and Anastasia Zolotarev
Photographer's Assistant Amy Bramble
Food Stylist Anastasia Zolotarev
Food Preparation Breda Fenn and Elena Zolotarev
Prop Stylist Jessica Hanson and Tess Thyregod
Head of Production Stephen Lang
Production Manager Sabeena Atchia

Colour reproduction by F1

Printed in China by C&C Offset Printing Co., Ltd.

The authorised representative in the EEA is Penguin Random House
Ireland, Morrison Chambers, 32 Nassau Street, Dublin D02 YH68.

Penguin Random House is committed to a sustainable future for our
business, our readers and our planet. This book is made from Forest
Stewardship Council® certified paper.